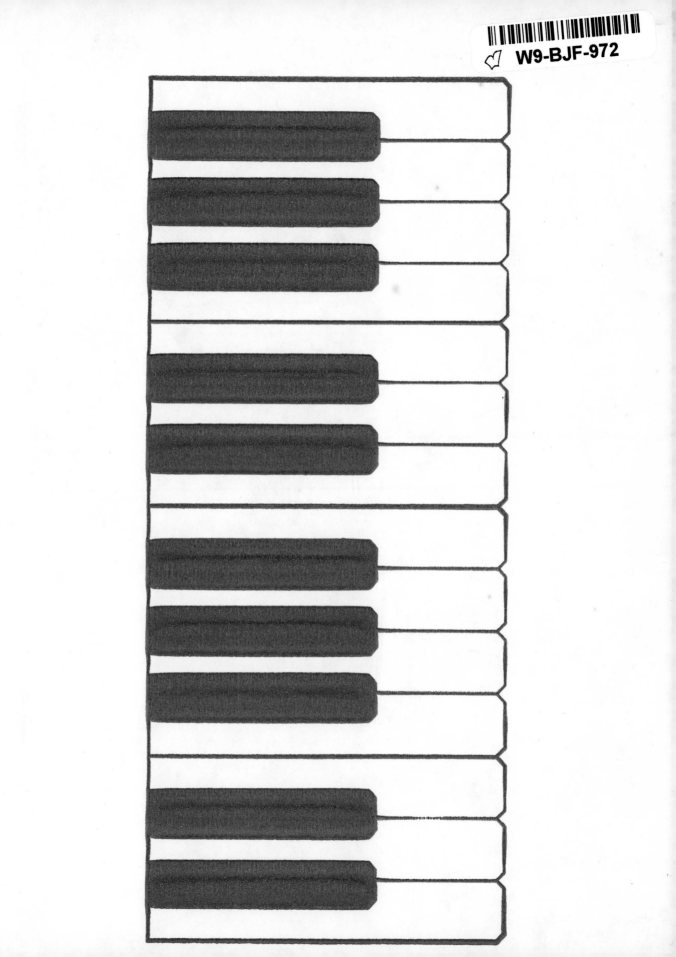

SILVER · BURDETT
music

ELIZABETH CROOK
BENNETT REIMER
DAVID S. WALKER

SILVER BURDETT COMPANY

MORRISTOWN, NEW JERSEY · GLENVIEW, ILLINOIS
PALO ALTO · DALLAS · ATLANTA

SPECIAL CONTRIBUTORS

William M. Anderson (non-Western music), Aurora, Ohio

Kojo Fosu Baiden (music of Africa), Silver Springs, Maryland

Dulce B. Bohn (recorder), Wilmington, Delaware

Charles L. Boilès (music of Mexico), Bloomington, Indiana

Ian L. Bradley (Canadian music), Victoria, British Columbia, Canada

Gerald Burakoff (recorder), Levittown, New York

Henry Burnett (music of Japan), Flushing, Long Island, New York

Richard J. Colwell (testing and evaluation), Urbana, Illinois

Marilyn C. Davidson (music for Orff instruments), Bergenfield, New Jersey

Joan Davies (music of Canada and Japan), Charlottetown, P.E.I., Canada

Kay Hardesty (special education), Chautauqua, New York

James M. Harris (music in early childhood), San Francisco, California

Doris E. Hays (avant-garde music), New York City

Nazir A. Jairazbhoy (music of India), Windsor, Ontario, Canada

Maria Jordan (music of Greece), Hicksville, Long Island, New York

Robert A. Kauffman (music of Africa), Seattle, Washington

Edna Knock (music of Canada), Brandon, Manitoba, Canada

John Lidstone (visual arts), Brooklyn, New York

David McHugh (youth music), New York City

Alan P. Merriam (music of the North American Indians), Bloomington, Indiana

Lucille Mitchell (American folk songs), Alexandria, Virginia

Maria Luisa Muñoz (music of Puerto Rico), Houston, Texas

Lynn Freeman Olson (listening program), New York City

Mary E. Perrin (music in the inner city), Chicago, Illinois

Carmino Ravosa (children's song literature), Briarcliff Manor, New York

Joyce Bogusky Reimer (avant-garde music), Wilmette, Illinois

Geraldine Slaughter (music of Africa), Washington, D.C.

Mark Slobin (music of the Near East), Middletown, Connecticut

Ruth Marie Stone (music of Africa), New York City

Leona B. Wilkins (music in the inner city), Evanston, Illinois

CONSULTANTS

Lynn Arizzi (levels 1 and 2), Reston, Virginia

Joy Browne (levels 5 and 6), Kansas City, Missouri

Nancy Crump, classroom teacher, Alexandria, Louisiana

Lyla Evans, classroom teacher, South Euclid, Ohio

Catherine Gallas, classroom teacher, Bridgeton, Missouri

Linda Haselton, classroom teacher, Westminster, California

Ruth A. Held, classroom teacher, Lancaster, Pennsylvania

Judy F. Jackson, classroom teacher, Franklin, Tennessee

Mary E. Justice, Auburn University, Auburn, Alabama

Jean Lembke (levels 3 and 4), Tonawanda, New York

Barbara Nelson, classroom teacher, Baytown, Texas

Terry Philips (youth music), New York City

Ruth Red, Director of Music Education, Houston, Texas

Mary Ann Shealy (levels 1 and 2), Florence, South Carolina

Beatrice Schattschneider (levels 1–6), Morristown, New Jersey

Paulette Schmalz, classroom teacher, Phoenix, Arizona

Sister Helen C. Schneider, Clarke College, Dubuque, Iowa

Merrill Staton (recordings), Alpine, New Jersey

ACKNOWLEDGMENTS

The authors and editors of SILVER BURDETT MUSIC acknowledge with gratitude the contributions of the following persons.

Marjorie Hahn, New York
Yoriko Kozumi, Japan
Ruth Merrill, Texas
Bennie Mae Oliver, Texas
Joanne Ryan, New York
Helen Spiers, Virginia
Mary Ann Nelson, Texas
Shirley Ventrone, Rhode Island
Avonelle Walker, New York

Credit and appreciation are due publishers and copyright owners for use of the following.

"April Fool's Day" by Marnie Pomeroy from POEMS FOR SEASONS AND CELEBRATIONS, edited by William Cole. © 1961 World Publishing Company, Cleveland, Ohio

"Blum" reprinted by permission of G. P. Putnam's Sons from Here, There and Everywhere by Dorothy Aldis. Copyright © 1928, 1956 by Dorothy Aldis.

"But You Are Mine" ("Lullaby") used by permission of Institute of African Studies, University of Ghana, Legon, Ghana

"Lewis Has a Trumpet" from IN THE MIDDLE OF THE TREES by Karla Kuskin. Copyright © 1958 by Karla Kuskin. By permission of Harper & Row, Publishers, Inc.

"Paper I" from THE COMPLETE POEMS OF CARL SANDBURG, copyright 1950 by Carl Sandburg; renewed 1978 by Margaret Sandburg, Helga Sandburg Crile and Janet Sandburg. Reprinted (or recorded) by permission of Harcourt Brace Jovanovich, Inc.

"Rain Sizes" from THE REASON FOR THE PELICAN by John Ciardi. Poem Copyright 1959 by The Curtis Publishing Company. By permission of J. B. Lippincott, Publishers.

CONTENTS

"I Clap My Hands"

Show rhythm by playing.

If you can move
to the steady beat,
you are ready to play
the steady beat.

Which way will you choose?

Which part will you play?

steady beat

quarter notes

eighth notes

eighth notes and quarter notes

Show direction in melody by singing.

MARCHING TO PRETORIA

DUTCH FOLK SONG FROM SOUTH AFRICA

ENGLISH WORDS BY JOSEF MARAIS
FROM SONGS FROM THE VELD, © 1942, G. SCHIRMER, INC. USED BY PERMISSION.

1. I'm with you and you're with me, And so we are all to-geth-er,
2. We have food, the food is good, And so we will eat to-geth-er,

So we are all to-geth-er, So we are all to-geth-er.
So we will eat to-geth-er, So we will eat to-geth-er.

Sing with me, I'll sing with you, And so we will sing to-geth-er,
When we eat, 'twill be a treat, And so let us sing to-geth-er,

As we march a-long.
As we march a-long.

REFRAIN

We are march-ing to Pre-to-ri-a, _____

Pre-to-ri-a, _____ Pre-to-ri-a, _____

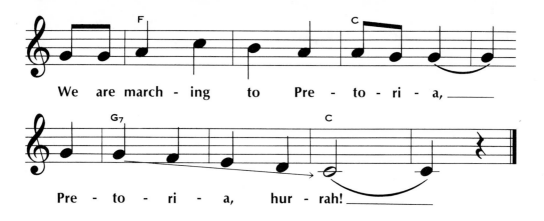

We are march - ing to Pre - to - ri - a, _____

Pre - to - ri - a, hur - rah! _____

Show direction in melody by playing.

Start on G and play down to C.

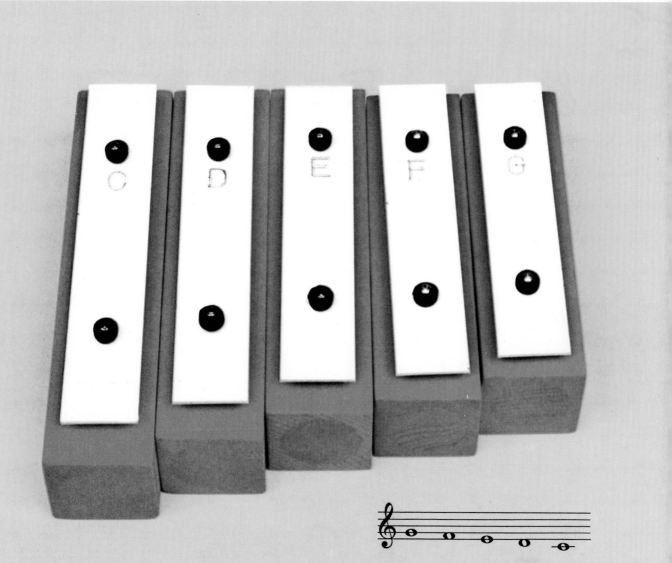

Show direction in melody by singing.

Listen to a melody to discover whether the ending moves

upward,

or downward.

BROTHER NOAH

AMERICAN SEA SONG

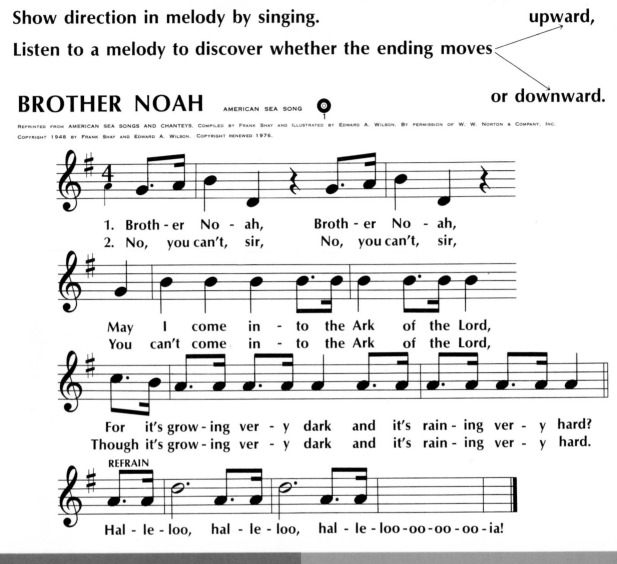

1. Broth - er No - ah,   Broth - er No - ah,
2. No,   you can't, sir,   No,   you can't, sir,

May   I   come   in - to   the   Ark   of   the   Lord,
You   can't come   in - to   the   Ark   of   the   Lord,

For   it's grow - ing ver - y   dark   and   it's rain - ing ver - y   hard?
Though it's grow - ing ver - y   dark   and   it's rain - ing ver - y   hard.

REFRAIN

Hal - le - loo,   hal - le - loo,   hal - le - loo - oo - oo - oo - ia!

Follow the notes as you sing.

Find the notes that show the missing part.

Do you see what you hear?

6

Show direction in melody by playing.

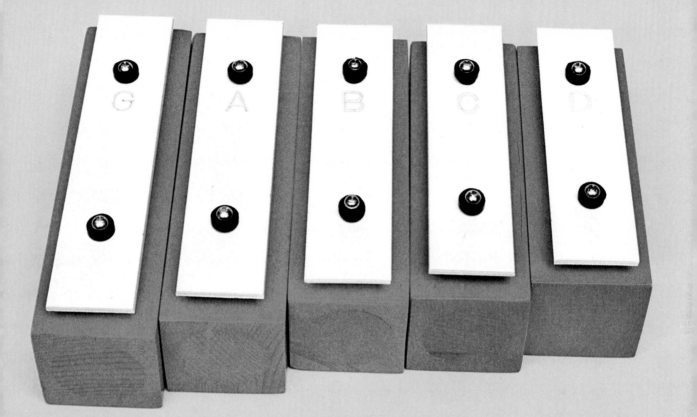

Play the ending of a song you know on the bells.

Start on high D and play down to G.

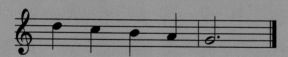

Which bells play *high* tones?

Which bells play *low* tones?

Draw notes for *high* tones on a staff.

Draw notes for *low* tones on a staff.

Listen to upward and downward direction.

OLD JOE CLARK
AMERICAN FOLK SONG   WORDS BY RAYMOND MATTHEWS

1. Old Joe Clark, he built a house, Took him 'bout a week;

He built the floors a - bove his head, The ceil - ings un - der his feet.

REFRAIN

Rock - a - rock, Old Joe Clark, Rock - a - rock, I'm gone;

Rock - a - rock, Old Joe Clark, Good - by, Lu - cy Long.

2. Old Joe Clark, he had a dog
   Like none you've ever seen;
   With floppy ears and curly tail,
   And six feet in between. *Refrain*

3. Old Joe Clark, he had a wife,
   Her name was Betty Sue;
   She had two great big brown eyes,
   The other two were blue. *Refrain*

PITY THE POOR PATAT

WORDS AND MUSIC BY JOSEF MARAIS. (ASCAP)

MELODY BASED ON AN AFRICAN FOLK TUNE

1. The tree, he has a bark,
A bark that's thick or thin.
Pit - y ____ the poor pa - tat,
He's on - ly got a skin.

2. The tree, he has his trunk,
He stares up in the sky.
Pity the poor patat,
He can't see with his eye.

3. The tree, he has his leaves,
They're waving all around.
Pity the poor patat,
For he lives in the ground.

4. Although the tree is proud,
He only gives us wood,
But from the poor patat
We get our daily food.

Bells

He's on - ly got a skin.
D   C   B   A   G

THE TREE IN THE WOOD

FOLK SONG FROM ENGLAND

1. All in___ a___ wood there grew a tree,
2. And on___ this___ tree there grew a limb,

The fin - est___ tree you ev - er did see;
The fin - est___ limb you ev - er did see;

The tree was in the wood,
The limb was on the tree, The tree was in the wood,

And the green leaves grew all a-round, a-round, a-round,

And the green leaves grew all a-round.

Repeat for additional lines in verses 3–8.

3. And on this limb there was a branch,

   The finest branch you ever did see;

   The branch was on the limb,

   The limb was on the tree,

   The tree was in the wood,

   And the green leaves grew . . .

4. And on this branch there was a nest, . . .

5. And in this nest there was an egg, . . .

6. And in this egg there was a bird, . . .

7. And on this bird there was a wing, . . .

8. And on this wing there was a feather, . . .

JOIN INTO THE GAME
WORDS AND MUSIC BY PAUL CAMPBELL

1. Let ev - 'ry - one clap hands like me. *(clap hands)*
2. Let ev - 'ry - one whis - tle like me. *(whistle)*

Let ev - 'ry - one clap hands like me. *(clap hands)*
Let ev - 'ry - one whis - tle like me. *(whistle)*

REFRAIN

Come on and join in - to the game;_____
Come on and join in - to the game;_____

You'll find that it's al - ways the same. *(clap hands)*
You'll find that it's al - ways the same. *(whistle)*

3. Let ev'ryone laugh like me, *(laugh)*

4. Let ev'ryone sneeze like me, *(sneeze)*

5. Let ev'ryone yawn like me, *(yawn)*

6. Let ev'ryone do what he wants, *(various sounds)*

How do the pictures show different sections?

ROLL AN' ROCK

BLACK SPIRITUAL

Oh, tell me,___ Mar-tha,___ Mar-tha, won't you tell me,

Where have___ you been so long?

Been a-roll-in' an' a-rock-in' at the old church gate,

An' my soul wants to go home to glo-ry.

Show that you hear different sections in music.

Roll an' rock,____ come a - long,____

Roll an' rock ____ all day long.____

Roll an' rock,____ come a - long,____

My soul wants to go home____ to glo - ry.

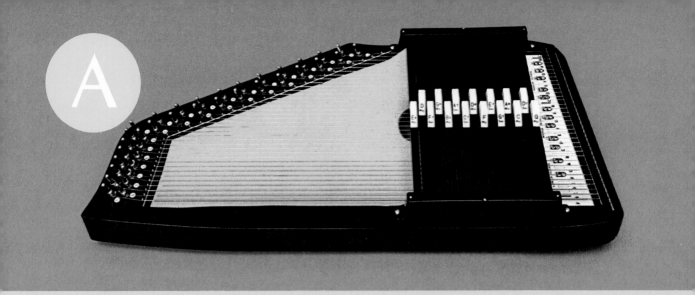

Autoharp

B

Show form by playing.

Drum

OLD DAN TUCKER

AMERICAN FOLK SONG

Old Dan Tuck - er was a might - y man,

He washed his face in the fry - ing pan,

Combed his hair with a wag - on wheel,

Had a tooth - ache in his heel;

So get out the way, Old Dan Tuck - er;

Get out the way, Old Dan Tuck - er;

Get out the way, Old Dan Tuck - er,

You're too late to get your sup - per.

Show form by playing and singing.

OLD TANTE KOBA

WORDS AND MUSIC BY JOSEF MARAIS. (ASCAP)

A VERSE

1. Old Tan - te Ko - ba she ought to know,
2. Old Tan - te Ko - ba she loves to eat,

She stirs her cof - fee with her own big toe.
She got so fat____ she can't see her feet.

Old Tan - te Ko - ba she is so dumb,
Old Tan - te Ko - ba she eats a - lone,

She thinks it's bet - ter than to use her thumb.
So no one knows____ that she nibbles the bone.

B REFRAIN

'Tis - n't my af - fair,____ 'tis - n't your af - fair,____

It's Tan - te Ko - ba's trou - bles so we need - n't care.

'Tis - n't my af - fair,____ 'tis - n't your af - fair,____

It's Tan - te Ko - ba's trou - bles so we need - n't care.

Instruments have tone color.
When you hear an instrument
you know, point to its picture.

claves

drum

guitar

cowbell

maracas

Each instrument has its own special sound,

or *tone color*, that you can hear.

Instrumental Parts for "Mama Paquita"

"Mama Paquita" ◎

MAMA PAQUITA

CARNIVAL SONG FROM BRAZIL   ENGLISH WORDS BY MARGARET MARKS

1. Ma - ma Pa - qui - ta,   Ma - ma Pa - qui - ta,

Ma - ma Pa - qui - ta, buy your ba - by a pa - pa - ya,

A ripe pa-pa-ya and a ba-na-na,

A ripe ba-na-na that your ba-by will en-joy, ma-ma-ma-ma,

Ma-ma Pa-qui-ta, Ma-ma Pa-qui-ta,

Ma-ma Pa-qui-ta says, "I have-n't an-y mon-ey

To buy pa-pa-yas and ripe ba-na-nas,

Let's go to Car-ni-val and dance the night a-way!"

2. Mama Paquita, Mama Paquita,

Mama Paquita, buy your baby some pajamas,

Some new pajamas, and a sombrero,

A new sombrero that your baby will enjoy, ma-ma-ma-ma,

Mama Paquita, Mama Paquita,

Mama Paquita says, "I haven't any money

To buy pajamas and a sombrero,

Let's go to Carnival and dance the night away!"

Voices have tone color.

Add the tone color of your own voice as you follow the notes.

MICHIE BANJO

CREOLE BAMBOULA   ENGLISH WORDS BY MARGARET MARKS

Look at Mich-ie Ban-jo, Fan-cy Mich-ie Ban-jo,

Strut-tin'___ down the street.

Fine

1. *Cha-peau*___ cocked on one
2. Dia-mond___ pin in his

side, Mich-ie Ban-jo, High but-ton shoes that squeak,
tie, Mich-ie Ban-jo, Bright yel-low gloves so neat,

Walk-in' stick a-swing-in' wide, Mich-ie Ban-jo,
Trou-sers pleat-ed way up high, Mich-ie Ban-jo,

D.C. al Fine

Ev-'ry-thing's all com-plete.
Ev-'ry-thing's all com-plete.

BUT THE CAT CAME BACK

WORDS AND MUSIC BY JOSEF MARAIS, (ASCAP)

Ⓐ VERSE

1. Fred-die Wil-son had a cat that he did-n't want to keep.

He of-fered him for free and he tried to sell him cheap.

He called up-on the preach-er one Sun-day for ad-vice;

The preach-er said, "Yes, leave him here, it would be so nice!"

B REFRAIN

But the cat came back, he would-n't stay a-way,

He was sit-ting on the porch on the ver-y next day.

The cat came back, he did-n't want to roam,

The ver-y next day it was "Home, Sweet Home."

2. Freddie put him on a ship and they headed for Ceylon.

   The ship was overloaded more than twenty thousand ton.

   Not far away from shore the cargo ship went down,

   There wasn't any doubt about it, everybody drowned. *Refrain*

3. Then he put the cat aboard with a man in a balloon,

   Who would give the cat away to the man in the moon.

   The balloon it didn't rise, it burst in bits instead,

   And ten miles from the spot, they found the man stone dead. *Refrain*

LADY, COME

FOLK SONG FROM ENGLAND

La - dy, come, Can't you see?

John fell off the white oak tree.

Add harmony to melody by playing the Autoharp.

With the index finger of your left hand, press the G button.

With your right hand, play half notes. Strum the strings every

two beats.

repeat

Listen to a sound piece for Autoharp.

Then, make up a sound piece of your own.

◉ *Autoharp Sound Piece*

SOUND PIECE 1: Autoharp Design   DAVID S. WALKER

Explore ways of making new sounds on the Autoharp.

TRY	PLAY

TRY
- Plucking strings
- Strumming strings
- Playing with hard mallet
- Playing with soft mallet
- Playing with plastic pick
- Playing with felt pick
- Sliding a comb along strings
- Sliding a ruler along strings
- Tapping wood case
- Rubbing strings with fingertips

PLAY
- High sounds
- Low sounds
- Sounds from high to low
- Sounds from low to high
- Several high sounds together
- Several low sounds together
- Loud sounds
- Soft sounds
- Long sounds
- Short sounds

Can you play this notation on the Autoharp?

1. ↑ ↑ ↑

2. . . . . .

3. . . . . .↗

4. ↑ ↓ ↑

23

Add harmony to this song by playing chords on the Autoharp.

AIN'T GONNA RAIN
AMERICAN FOLK SONG

1. The wood-chuck, he's a - chop - pin' wood,

The pos - sum, he's a - haul - in'.

My poor old dog fell off a log And killed him - self a - bawl - in'.

REFRAIN

It ain't gon - na rain, it ain't gon - na rain, It ain't gon - na rain no more.

Come on down, ev - 'ry - bod - y sing. It ain't gon - na rain no more.

2. Just bake them biscuits good and brown,
   It ain't gonna rain no more.
   Swing your ladies round and round,
   It ain't gonna rain no more. *Refrain*

3. I'll tune the fiddle, you get the bow,
   It ain't gonna rain no more.
   The weatherman just told me so,
   It ain't gonna rain no more. *Refrain*

4. Oh, what did the blackbird say to the crow?
   "It ain't gonna rain no more.
   It ain't gonna hail, it ain't gonna snow,
   It ain't gonna rain no more." *Refrain*

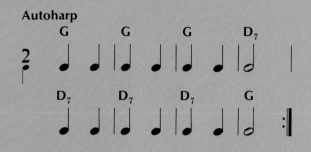

This song uses the G and D₇ chords.

Follow the letter names in the music.

SWEETLY SINGS THE DONKEY ROUND

Long ago, shepherds played pipes
that looked like these.

LOOK

LISTEN

Another kind of pipe is
called a *recorder*.
In the picture,
you see a
group of recorders.

Listen to them
play together.

Anonymous:
Dadme Albricias, Hijos d'Eva

You can play a pipe
called a
soprano recorder.

Hold the recorder
with both hands,
with the left hand
on top.

Cover-the-Hole Test

Press just hard enough
so the hole will make
a light mark on each
finger of your
left hand.

Making a Sound

Cover the tip of
the mouthpiece
with your lips.
Blow gently through
the recorder,
starting to blow with
a "daah."

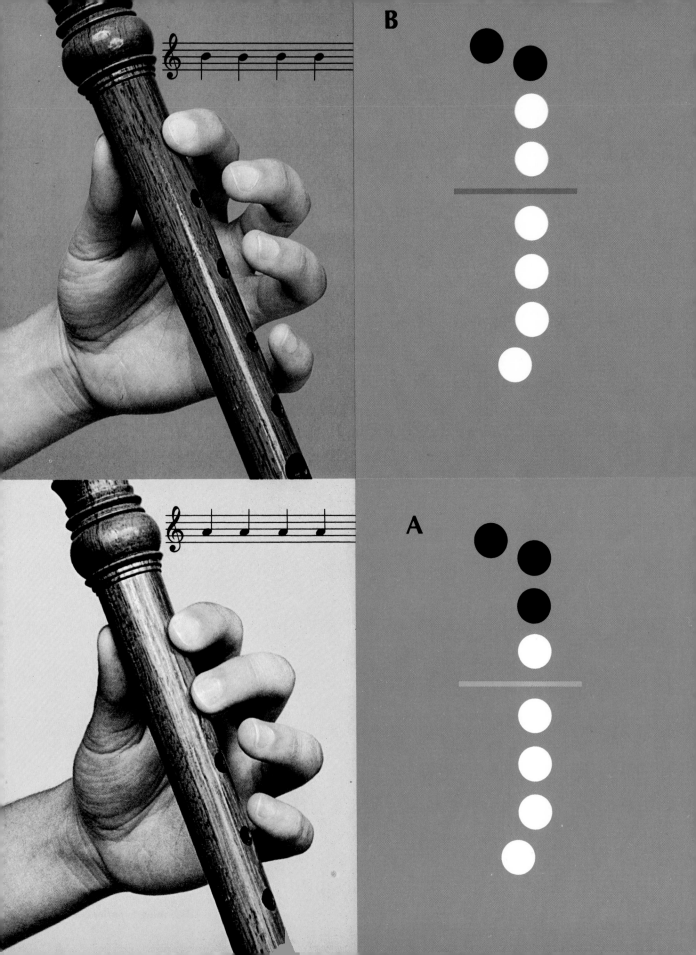

G

Look at the pictures to see which fingers you use
to play the tones B, A, and G.

Cover the holes with your fingers.
Now blow gently four times for each tone.
Start each blow with a "daah."

Can you find a sign that tells you where
the line G is on the staff?

Now you are ready to play
a part with the melody of
"Ain't Gonna Rain."
Your part is
a countermelody.

Recorder

Use B A G with songs you know.

1. Fill in the silences in "Mama Paquita,"
playing

G G G   G A G

2. Play this pattern throughout "Lady, Come."

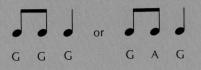

3. Play G throughout the first section of "Marching to Pretoria,"
using

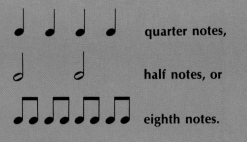

quarter notes,

half notes, or

eighth notes.

4. Play a countermelody with "Brother Noah."

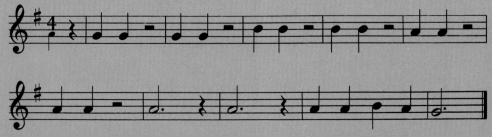

Use B A G to play these melodies.

LULLABY FRENCH FOLK MELODY

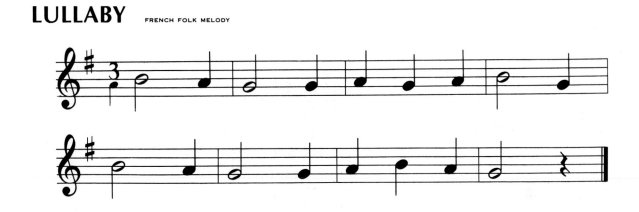

HOP, OLD SQUIRREL BLACK-AMERICAN SINGING GAME

SING TOGETHER

OLD ENGLISH ROUND

I Sing, sing to-geth - er, Mer - ri - ly, mer - ri - ly sing;

II Sing, sing to-geth - er, Mer - ri - ly, mer - ri - ly sing;

Sing, sing, sing, sing.

1. A melody sung alone has no harmony.

2. A melody with chords has harmony.

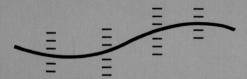

3. A melody sung as a round has harmony.

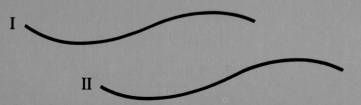

I

II

Sing "A Ram Sam Sam" with *no* harmony.

Add Autoharp chords for harmony.

A RAM SAM SAM   FOLK SONG FROM MOROCCO

Which of these pieces of music has harmony?

Which has no harmony?

Smith: *Three Brevities for Solo Flute*

Sor: *Variations on a Theme by Mozart*

Do you hear harmony, or no harmony, in this song?

CHE CHE KOOLAY SINGING GAME FROM GHANA

FROM HI, NEIGHBOR (BOOK 2) BY UNITED STATES FOR UNICEF, UNITED NATIONS, N.Y. USED BY PERMISSION.

2

LEADER

(Hands on head)   Che-che koo-lay

(Hands on shoulders)   Che-che ko-fee sa

(Hands on hips)   Ko-fee sa-lan-ga

(Hands on knees)   Ka-ka-shee lan-ga

(Grasp ankles)   Koom-ma-dye-day

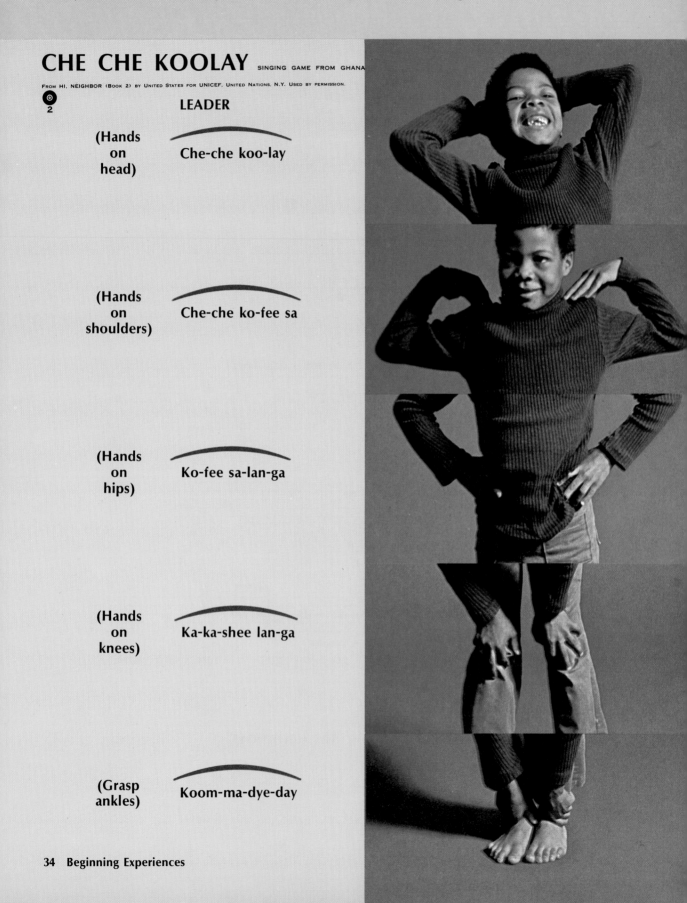

Follow the phrases as you sing. Are they the same length, or different?

As you play the game, feel the length of each phrase.

GROUP

Che-che koo-lay

Che-che ko-fee sa

Ko-fee sa-lan-ga

Ka-ka-shee lan-ga

Koom-ma-dye-day

What part of this painting seems to be lively and active?
What part seems to have little or no movement?

Listen to these two pieces of music. In one, the
music is mostly still. In the other, it is active.

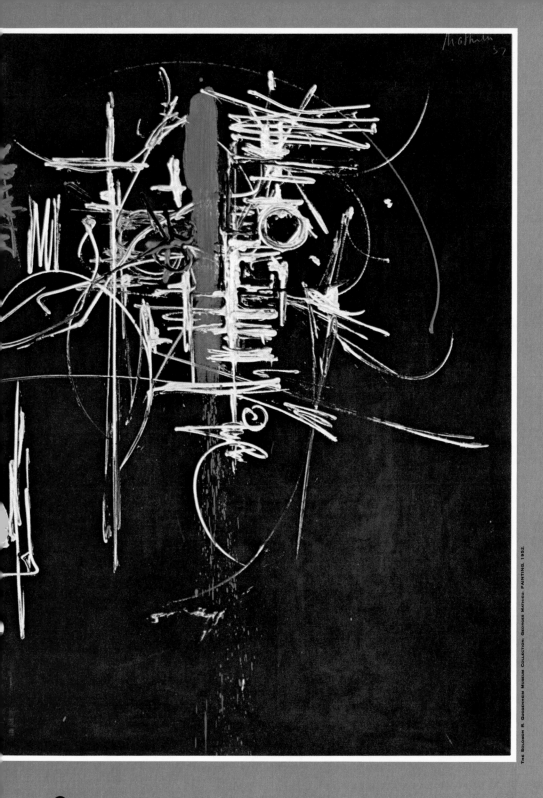

Stravinsky: *A Soldier's Tale Suite,* "The Royal March"

Stravinsky: *A Soldier's Tale Suite,* "Music to Scene II"

You *see* things in a painting all at once.

You *hear* things in music over a span of time.

What are these

children

hearing?

They are hearing the *sounds*.

How do you hear sounds?

You hear sounds with your *ears*.

Think of what you hear in "Kites Are Fun."

A group sings the song. There are both

men's and women's voices in the group.

The voices are accompanied by a variety of

instruments.

The music has a steady beat. | | | | | |

The music has both long and short sounds.

      The more sounds your ears hear—

      The more sounds you think about—

      The more sounds you feel.

◎ Dedrick, Chris: *Kites Are Fun*
2

Listen to two recordings of this song.
Which is *fast?* Which is *slow?*

OH, WHAT A BEAUTIFUL CITY

BLACK SPIRITUAL

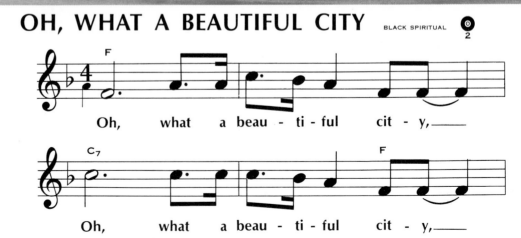

Oh,   what   a beau - ti - ful   cit - y, ——

Oh,   what   a beau - ti - ful   cit - y, ——

Sing the song both ways.

Which *tempo* feels right to you?

Which conductor chooses a *faster tempo* for this piece?

Handel: *Water Music,* "Air"

Oh, what a beau - ti - ful cit - y,___

Twelve gates - a to the cit - y,___ Hal - le - lu - jah!

In this song does the beat get slower, or faster, or stay the same?

HEY HO, HEY LO

SLOVAKIAN FOLK TUNE   ENGLISH WORDS BY RAYMOND MATTHEWS

Hey ho, hey lo, tam-bou-rines are ring - ing;

Hey ho, hey lo, ring - ing all a - round.

Lis - ten, lis - ten, hear them jin - gle jan - gle,

Mak - ing mu - sic with a hap - py sound.

Fast - er, fast - er, how they jin - gle jan - gle,

Mak - ing mu - sic with a hap - py sound.

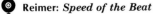 **Reimer:** *Speed of the Beat*

Does the beat get faster, or slower, in this song?

WIND UP THE APPLE TREE

AMERICAN SINGING GAME

FROM SINGING GAMES AND PLAYPARTY GAMES BY RICHARD CHASE, DOVER PUBLICATIONS, INC., NEW YORK, 1949, 1967.
REPRINTED THROUGH THE PERMISSION OF THE PUBLISHER.

Wind up the ap-ple tree! Hold on tight!

Wind it all__ day__ and wind it all__ night!

Faster

Stir up the dump-lings, the pot boils o-ver!

Can you hear the beat change in this music?

Ibert: *Entr-acte*

Can you hear the beat stop and hold in this song? Can you find the sign that tells you when to stop and hold?

CARROT STEW

WORDS AND MUSIC BY LARRY GROCE

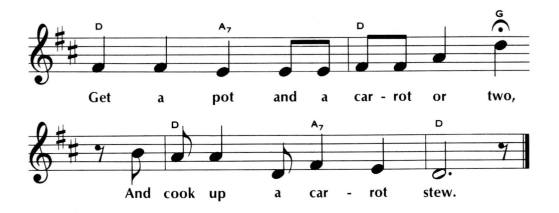

Get a pot and a car - rot or two,

And cook up a car - rot stew.

2. Nothing makes our tummies so full
   And keeps us happy too,
   As a great big pot or a little bitty bowl
   Or a spoonful of carrot stew. *Refrain*

3. So when you come to our little house,
   Bring a carrot if you have a few.
   We'll put it in a pot 'til it's nice and hot,
   And make some carrot stew. *Refrain*

Try these jump-rope chants at recess. Will you jump fast, or slow?

Hana, mana, mona, mike,
Barcelona, bona, strike,
Hare, ware, frown, venac,
Harrico, warrico, we, wo, wac.

Down by the ocean,
Down by the sea,
Johnnie broke a milk bottle
And blamed it on me.
I told Ma and Ma told Pa.
Johnnie got a licking
With a Ha! Ha! Ha!
How many licks did he get?
1, 2, 3, etc.

Play a tambourine on every beat.

Find the sign that tells you when to stop and hold.

ALOUETTE
FOLK SONG FROM CANADA

REFRAIN

A - lou - et - te, gen - tille A - lou - et - te,

A - lou - et - te, je te plu - me - rai.

1. Je te plu - me - rai la tête, Je te plu - me - rai la tête,
2. Je te plu - me - rai la bec, Je te plu - me - rai la bec,

(No repeat first time)

1. Et la tête, et la tête.
2. {Et la bec, et la bec. A - lou-ette, A - lou-ette. Oh!
   {Et la tête, et la tête.

3. Le nez   4. Le dos   5. Les pattes   6. Le cou

Listen to this music. Circle the word that best describes what is happening to the beat.

Is it fast, or slow? Is it getting faster, or getting slower?

1.	FAST	SLOW
2.	GETTING FASTER	GETTING SLOWER
3.	FAST	SLOW
4.	FAST	SLOW
5.	GETTING FASTER	GETTING SLOWER

Train Ride

Now listen to the music on this recording.

Circle the word that best describes the tempo.

Is it fast, or slow? Do you hear the beat stop and hold?

If you do, circle ⌒. If you do not, circle NO ⌒.

1.	FAST	SLOW	⌒	NO ⌒
2.	FAST	SLOW	⌒	NO ⌒
3.	FAST	SLOW	⌒	NO ⌒
4.	FAST	SLOW	⌒	NO ⌒

Beethoven: *Violin Concerto,* "Rondo"
Alouette

Chopin: *Sonata in B^b Minor,* "Funeral March"
Haydn: *Quartet in D Minor,* Movement 4

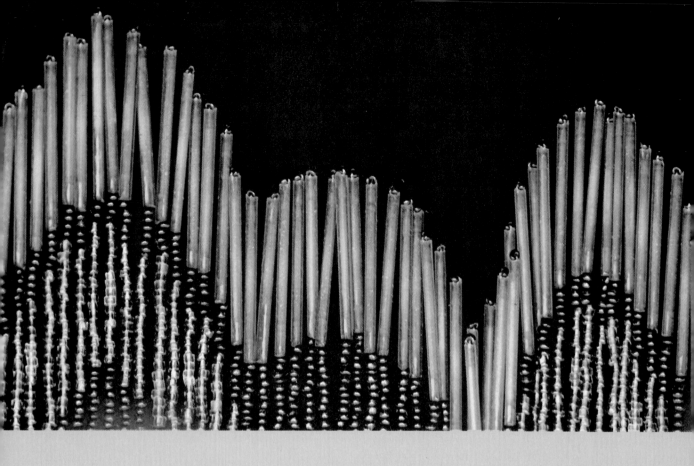

Choose a box
and trace the arrows.
Play a swooping sound
on the bells or on the keyboard
in the same direction
as the arrows.

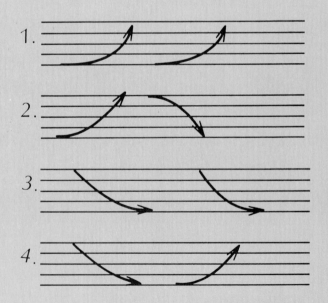

Follow the lines as you hear the sound moving upward and downward on the recording.

🔊 _Electronic Sounds 1 and 2_

Do you see what you hear? Which line shows what you hear next?

🔊 _Hearing Electronic Sounds_

Follow the notes to discover direction in this song. Does the ending of each phrase move upward, or downward?

ALL THE PRETTY LITTLE HORSES

FOLK SONG FROM SOUTHERN UNITED STATES

COLLECTED, ADAPTED AND ARRANGED BY JOHN A. LOMAX & ALAN LOMAX TRO-© COPYRIGHT 1934 AND RENEWED 1962 LUDLOW MUSIC, INC., NEW YORK, N.Y. USED BY PERMISSION.

Hush - a - by, don't you cry, Go to sleep-y, lit - tle ba - by.

When you wake, you shall have All the pret-ty lit - tle hors - es:

Blacks and bays, dap-ples and grays, Coach and six - a lit-tle hors - es.

Hush - a - by, don't you cry, Go to sleep-y, lit-tle ba - by.

Play B A G on the bells.

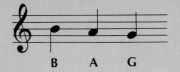

B   A   G

Play it fast. Play it slow.

Play it in this pattern.

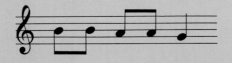

CLOVER

FOLK SONG FROM CZECHOSLOVAKIA   ENGLISH WORDS BY RAYMOND MATTHEWS

1. Clo - ver's grow - ing here;   Clo - ver's grow - ing there.

Now the win - ter's o - ver, Fields are green with clo - ver

Grow - ing ev - 'ry - where.   Now the win - ter's o - ver,

Fields are green with clo - ver Grow - ing ev - ry - where.

2. Clover smells so sweet. (*2 times*)

When the day is fair,

Its fragrance fills the air, } (*2 times*)

The clover smells so sweet.

3. Clover has three leaves. (*2 times*)

If a fourth one's there,

You'll find it's very rare, } (*2 times*)

For clover has three leaves.

50 Melody

Follow the upward and downward direction of the notes in this melody as you listen to the recording.

PIPE IN D MAJOR ALBERT ROUSSEL

SKIN AND BONES

FOLK SONG FROM KENTUCKY   COLLECTED BY JEAN RITCHIE

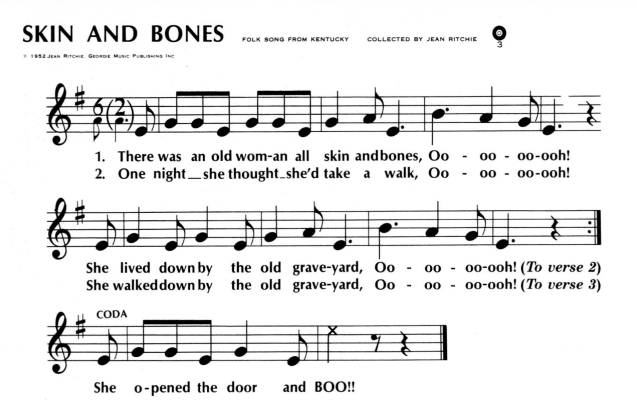

1. There was an old wom-an all skin and bones, Oo - oo - oo-ooh!
2. One night __ she thought __ she'd take a walk, Oo - oo - oo-ooh!

She lived down by the old grave-yard, Oo - oo - oo-ooh! (*To verse 2*)
She walked down by the old grave-yard, Oo - oo - oo-ooh! (*To verse 3*)

CODA

She o-pened the door and BOO!!

3. She saw the bones a-layin' around,

   Oo-oo-oo-ooh!

   She went to the closet to get a broom,

   Oo-oo-oo-ooh!   (*To coda*)

Play this pattern on the bells every time it comes in the song.

B   A   G   E

To play the pattern on the recorder, you need a new note, E. Look on page 53 to discover how to play it.

E

Recorder or Bells

E   B A G

You can play this song on bells or recorder.

Follow the direction of the melody as you play.

CHICKA HANKA AMERICAN FOLK SONG

FROM ECHOES OF AFRICA IN FOLK SONGS OF THE AMERICAS, BY BEATRICE LANDECK. COPYRIGHT © 1961, BY BEATRICE LANDECK. PUBLISHED BY DAVID McKAY COMPANY, INC. REPRINTED BY PERMISSION.

Cap - tain,   go side - track your train!___

Cap - tain,   go side - track your train!___

Num-ber Three in line,   Com - in'   in   on   time,

Cap - tain,   go side - track your train!___

Here are parts of songs to play on bells.

Follow the direction of the melody as you play.

1.   2.

- loo - oo - oo - oo - ia!   Pre - to - ri - a,   hur - rah!

3.

It ain't gon-na rain no more.

4.

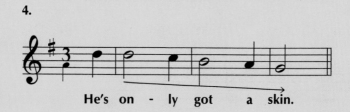

He's on - ly got a skin.

5.

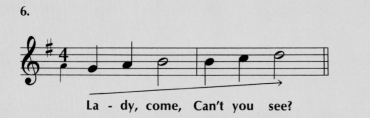

Go to sleep-y lit - tle ba - by.

6.

Lady, come, Can't you see?

7.

Oo - oo - oo - ooh!

8.

Car - ni - val and dance the night a - way!

9.

All in___ a___ wood there grew a tree,

ON THE FIRST THANKSGIVING DAY

MUSIC BY JAKOB HINTZE

WORDS TRADITIONAL

On the first Thanks - giv - ing Day,

Pil - grims went to church to pray,

Thanked the Lord for sun and rain,

Thanked him for the fields of grain.

Now Thanks - giv - ing comes a - gain:

Praise the Lord as they did then.

Thank him for the sun and rain,

Thank him for the fields of grain.

WHAT DO YOU HEAR? 2: MELODY 🎵

Listen to these pieces of music.

As each number is called, circle the word that best describes the direction the melody is moving. Is it moving *upward,* **or** *downward,* **or both** *upward* **and** *downward?*

---

1. *UPWARD   DOWNWARD*
   UPWARD AND DOWNWARD

---

2. *UPWARD   DOWNWARD*
   UPWARD AND DOWNWARD

---

3. *UPWARD   DOWNWARD*
   UPWARD AND DOWNWARD

Beethoven: *Concerto No. 5 in E^b Major,* "Emperor," Movement 1

---

1. *UPWARD   DOWNWARD*

---

2. *UPWARD   DOWNWARD*

---

3. *UPWARD   DOWNWARD*

---

4. *UPWARD   DOWNWARD*

Gershwin: *Rhapsody in Blue*
Poncielli: *Dance of the Hours*
Rimsky-Korsakov: *Le Coq D'or*
Kuhlah: *Sonatina*

Here are four composers.

On the recording, you will hear one of them tell you

what a composer does.

Things People Do with Music

RAIN SONG

WORDS AND MUSIC BY DAVID McHUGH © 1972 DAVID McHUGH

The rain just keeps on fall-ing, And the sky is col-ored grey;

The birds don't stop their sing-ing ___ 'Cause it's just an-oth-er day;

And the clouds keep pass-ing o-ver, Bring-in' rain to flow'rs be-low;

While the sun keeps wait-ing pa-tient-ly To un-veil its gold-en glow;

Some-times sun shines, and oth-er times it rains; ___

But to me it's all the same, ___

To me it's all the same. ___

When you bounce and catch a ball, you make motions in sets of two.
In music, these sets are called *meter.*

NEW YEAR'S SONG

Kazoe-uta   FOLK SONG FROM JAPAN   ENGLISH VERSION BY ROSEMARY JACQUES

1. On the eve of New Year's,___ Bus - y peo-ple, hap-py peo - ple,
   Hi - to - tsu to ya,_____ Hi - to - yo a - ku - re - ba,

Run - ning here and there,   Run - ning here and there,
Ni - gi - ya - ka de,   Ni - gi - ya - ka de,

Dec - o - rate the bam-boo trees to cel - e -brate the day,_____
O - ka - za - ri ta - te - ta - ru ma - tsu - ka - za - ri,_____

Cel - e -brate the day.
Ma - tsu - ka - za - ri.

2. On the eve of New Year's,

   Paper streamers, fresh plum blossoms

   Hang above the door,

   Hang above the door,

   Telling all who pass by

     to have a happy day,

   Have a happy day.

3. On the day of New Year's,

   Games are played and songs are sung

   To celebrate the day,

   Celebrate the day.

   People come to wish each other

     Happy New Year's Day,

   Happy New Year's Day.

Recorder or Bells

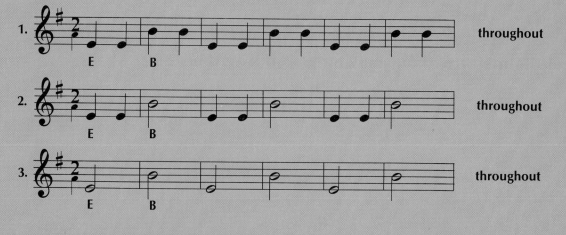

1. E B throughout

2. E B throughout

3. E B throughout

Woodblock

throughout

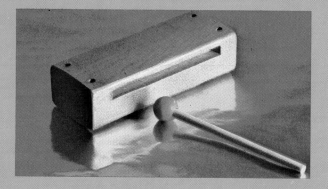

Gong

throughout

When you play the "Find the Ring" game,

you feel beats in sets of three.

Feel the meter without moving as you sing the song.

FIND THE RING

FOLK SONG FROM GREECE   ENGLISH WORDS BY MARIA JORDAN

1. Find the ring, the ring that keeps mov - ing,
2. Find the ring, the ring that keeps mov - ing,

Find the ring, oh, where did it go?
Find the ring of sil - ver or gold.

The se - cret ring's in some - bod - y's hand, Some -
Pass it to me, I'll pass it to you, We

bod - y you know, come guess if you can!
must - n't get caught, what - ev - er we do!

Don't say a word if you are the one, Don't

give it a - way and spoil all the fun!

Tambourine

$\frac{3}{}$ ♩ ♩ ♩♩|♩ ♩ ♩|♩ ♩ ♩|♩ ♩ :‖

Finger Cymbals

$\frac{3}{}$ ♩ ♩|♩ ♩|♩ ♩|♩ ♩|♩ :‖

Find the lines that separate the beats in sets of three.

These are called *bar lines*.

SANDY McNAB   ROUND

USED BY PERMISSION OF ANFOR MUSIC PUBLISHING COMPANY.

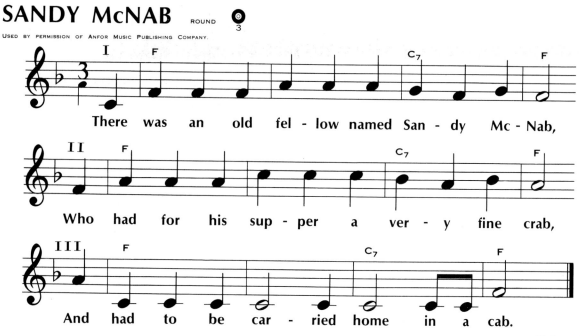

I

There was an old fel - low named San - dy Mc - Nab,

II

Who had for his sup - per a ver - y fine crab,

III

And had to be car - ried home in a cab.

You have sung, played, and heard music in different meters.

Listen to the recording.

As each number is called, look at the chart. It will help you hear the meter in sets of two and sets of three.

Kingsley: *Piece in Two Meters*

CALL CHART 1: METER

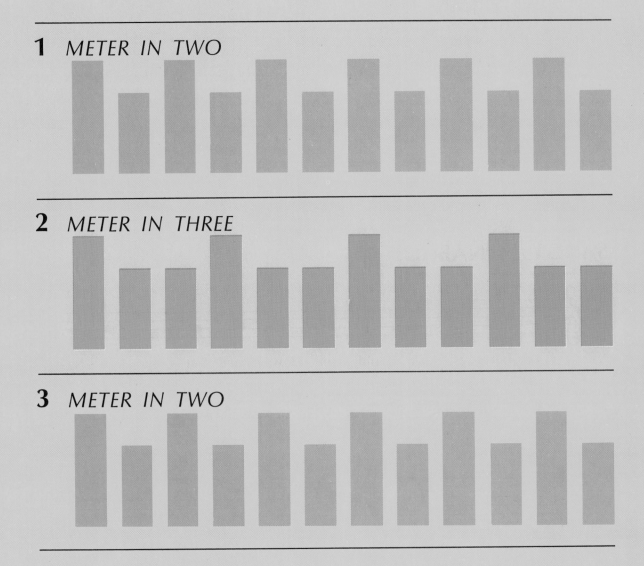

1 *METER IN TWO*

2 *METER IN THREE*

3 *METER IN TWO*

Feel the beats moving in sets of three as you listen to this song.

Play a tambourine in section B.

$\frac{3}{}$ ♩ ♩ ♩ | ♩ ♩ ♩ |

Hit shake shake Hit shake shake

Which of the three beats is the strongest?

Make up a tambourine part of your own.

BUYING FISH

YIDDISH FOLK SONG   ENGLISH WORDS BY ELIZABETH S. BACHMAN

VERSE

1. One day his moth - er sent him to mar - ket
2. Moth - er had said, "Go straight to the mar - ket;

To buy some fish_____ to fry._____
Don't lin - ger on _____ the way."

But when he got there he could - n't re - mem - ber
But he stopped to watch a game in the park, And

What kind she want - ed him to buy._____
now — oh, dear! what will Moth - er say?_____

REFRAIN

Day, day, day, day, day, day, Day, day, day, day, day, day,

Day, day, day, day, day, day, Day, day, day, day.

'TATERS

YIDDISH FOLK SONG   ENGLISH WORDS BY JACOB SLOAN

1. Sun - day, 'ta - ters, Mon - day, 'ta - ters,

Tues - day and Wednes - day,___ 'ta - ters,

Thurs - day and Fri - day,___ 'ta - ters,

Sab - bath, for a spe - cial treat, there's a 'ta - ter pud - ding!

Sun - day___ starts with___ 'ta - ters.

2. Bread and 'taters,

Meat and 'taters,

Lunch and dinner, 'taters.

Over and over, 'taters.

Once, for a special treat, there's a 'tater pudding!

Sunday starts with 'taters.

3. Still, 'taters,

Ever, 'taters,

Always, always, 'taters!

Today and tomorrow, 'taters!

After Sabbath pot roasts there's a 'tater pudding!

Sunday starts with 'taters.

GING GONG GOOLI

FOLK SONG FROM BRITISH GUIANA

Ging gong goo - li goo - li goo - li goo - li wat - cha,

Ging gong goo, ging gong goo.

Ging gong goo - li goo - li goo - li goo - li wat - cha,

Ging gong goo, ging gong goo.

Hai - la, _____ hai - la shai - la, _____

Shai - la hai - la shai - la ho - la - ho!

Hai - la, _____ hai - la shai - la, _____

Shai - la hai - la shai - la ho! _____

LOVE

WORDS AND MUSIC BY CARMINO RAVOSA © 1971 CARMINO RAVOSA

1. Love can charm the birds___ right out of the trees,

Love can take the hon-ey a-way from the bees;

Love can make a li-on stand up and say, "Please."___

2. Love can turn a hurricane into a breeze,

   Love can get a hermit to smile and say, "Cheese";

   Love can make a dog learn to live with his fleas.

3. Love can bring a giant right down to his knees,

   Love can make the North and the South Poles unfreeze;

   Love can make a kid learn to eat all his peas.

Recorder or Bells

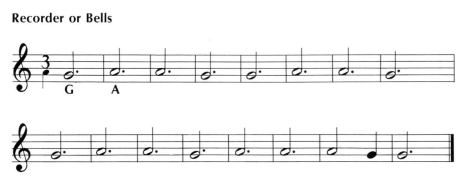

G   A

WHAT DO YOU HEAR? 3: METER ⦿

Each time a number is called, decide whether the beats are grouped in sets of two, or in sets of three.

If you think the beats are grouped in sets of two, draw a circle around METER IN 2.

If you think the beats are grouped in sets of three, draw a circle around METER IN 3.

Listen. Then circle what you hear.

1	METER IN 2	METER IN 3
2	METER IN 2	METER IN 3
3	METER IN 2	METER IN 3

Kingsley: *Piece in Two Meters*

1	METER IN 2	METER IN 3
2	METER IN 2	METER IN 3
3	METER IN 2	METER IN 3

Ton moulin

How would you read this poem?
Use loud and soft sounds to change
the dynamics.

RAIN SIZES

Rain comes in various sizes.
Some rain is as small as a mist.
It tickles your face with surprises,
And tingles as if you'd been kissed.

Some rain is the size of a sprinkle
And doesn't put out all the sun.
You can see the drops sparkle and twinkle,
And a rainbow comes out when it's done.

Some rain is as big as a nickle
And comes with a crash and a hiss.
It comes down too heavy to tickle.
It's more like a splash than a kiss.

When it rains the right size and you're
    wrapped in
Your rainclothes, it's fun out of doors.
But run home before you get trapped in
The big rain that rattles and roars.

John Ciardi

To change the dynamics in the
recording of this song, use the volume
knob on the record or cassette player.

THE GHOST OF JOHN

WORDS AND MUSIC BY MARTHA GRUBB

"POOR TOM" FROM ROUNDS. USED THROUGH COURTESY OF COOPERATIVE RECREATION SERVICE, INC., DELAWARE, OHIO.

Have you seen the ghost of John?

Long white bones with the skin all gone,_____

Oo,   Oo,_____

Would-n't it be chil - ly with no skin on!

Ibert: "Parade"

Add dynamics to a song you know.

Take turns playing a ringing instrument

to "The Ghost of John."

Which sign tells you to get louder? get softer?

1. 𝅗𝅥   𝅗𝅥 | 𝅘𝅥 𝅘𝅥 𝅗𝅥 |

2. 𝅝 | 𝅘𝅥 𝅘𝅥 𝅗𝅥 |

3. 𝅘𝅥 𝅘𝅥 𝅘𝅥 𝅘𝅥 | 𝅘𝅥 𝅘𝅥 𝅗𝅥 |

Notice that two quarter notes can take the place of a half note.

How many quarter notes can take the place of a whole note?

How many half notes can take the place of a whole note?

Low D

To play a recorder part for
"The Ghost of John," you need a
new note, low D.
When you can play low D,
try playing the bells or recorder
part at the top of page 73.

🔘 Grieg: "In the Hall of the Mountain King"
4

In this piece you will hear many changes of dynamics.

As each number is called, decide what dynamics you hear.

CALL CHART 2: DYNAMICS 🔘
4

---

1. *LOUD*

---

2. *SOFT*

---

3. *LOUD*

---

4. *GETTING SOFTER*

---

5. *GETTING LOUDER*

---

6. *LOUD*

Locke: *Saraband*

POLLY WOLLY DOODLE

AMERICAN FOLK SONG

1. Oh, I went down South for to see my Sal,
2. Oh, my Sal, she is a_____ maid - en fair,

Sing - ing Pol - ly Wol - ly Doo - dle all the day;
Sing - ing Pol - ly Wol - ly Doo - dle all the day;

My___ Sal, she is a___ spunk - y gal,
With___ curl - y eyes and___ laugh - ing hair,

Sing - ing Pol - ly Wol - ly Doo - dle all the day.
Sing - ing Pol - ly Wol - ly Doo - dle all the day.

REFRAIN

Fare thee well,___ fare thee well,___ Fare thee well my fair - y fay,___

For I'm goin' to Loui - si - an - a, For to see my Su - sy - an - na,

Sing - ing Pol - ly Wol - ly Doo - dle all the day.___

3. The partridge is a pretty bird,

   It has a speckled breast,

   It steals away the farmer's grain,

   And totes it to its nest! *Refrain*

4. The raccoon's tail is ringed around,

   The 'possum's tail is bare,

   The rabbit's got no tail at all,

   Just a little bitty bunch of hair! *Refrain*

SHEPHERD, SHEPHERD

BLACK SPIRITUAL

TAKEN FROM AMERICAN NEGRO SONGS AND SPIRITUALS BY JOHN W. WORK. © 1940 BY JOHN W. WORK. USED BY PERMISSION OF CROWN PUBLISHERS, INC.

1. Shep - herd, Shep - herd, where'd you lose your sheep?
2. Shep - herd, Shep - herd, where'd you leave your lambs?

Shep - herd, Shep - herd, where'd you lose your sheep?
Shep - herd, Shep - herd, where'd you leave your lambs?

Shep - herd, Shep - herd, where'd you lose your sheep?
Shep - herd, Shep - herd, where'd you leave your lambs?

O the sheep all gone a - stray,____
O the sheep all gone a - stray,____

The sheep all gone____ a - stray.
The sheep all gone____ a - stray.

Shostakovich: "Polka"

Mendelssohn: "Nocturne"

SOUND PIECE 2: Dynamic Design

DAVID S. WALKER

Can you discover how to play one of the instruments in Idea A?

Follow the color line. It will tell you when to play louder or softer.

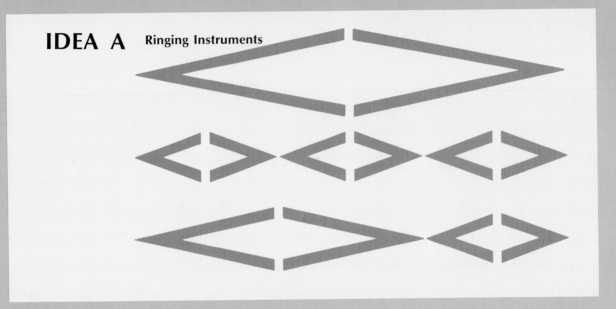

IDEA A Ringing Instruments

Notice when you play loud and soft in Idea B.

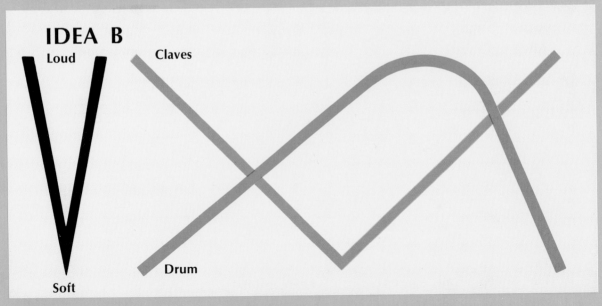

IDEA B

Loud

Claves

Soft

Drum

Play your part of the Sound Piece alone before playing it with others.

Make up your own Sound Piece using some of these ideas.

WHAT YOU GONNA CALL YOUR PRETTY LITTLE BABY?

BLACK SPIRITUAL

REFRAIN

What you gon - na call your pret - ty lit - tle ba - by,

What you gon - na call your pret - ty lit - tle ba - by,

What you gon - na call your pret - ty lit - tle ba - by,

Fine

Born, born in Beth - le - hem?___

1. Some say one thing, I'll say Im - man - uel,

D.C.

Born, born in Beth - le - hem.___

2. Some call Him one thing,
   I'll call Him Jesus,
   Born, born in Bethlehem.

3. Sweet little baby,
   Born in a manger,
   Born, born in Bethlehem.

PRAY GOD BLESS

ROUND FROM ENGLAND

Pray God bless all friends here,

A mer-ry, mer-ry Christ-mas and a hap-py New Year.

Choose one of these parts to play on bells or recorder.

Play the part all through "Pray God Bless."

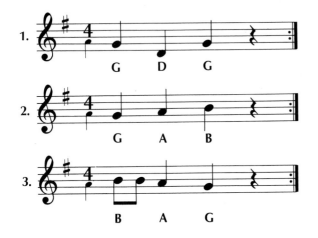

1. G D G

2. G A B

3. B A G

VALENTINE ROUND

WORDS ANONYMOUS   MUSIC BY DAVID EDDLEMAN

Do you love me, or do___ you___ not?

You told me once___ but___ I for-got!

WHAT DO YOU HEAR? 4: DYNAMICS ⊙4

Each time a number is called, decide what dynamics you hear and draw a circle around the correct word.

Listen. Then circle what you hear.

Locke: *Saraband*

LOUD	*SOFT*
LOUD	*SOFT*
LOUD	*SOFT*
GETTING LOUDER	*GETTING SOFTER*
GETTING LOUDER	*GETTING SOFTER*
LOUD	*SOFT*

There are many different styles of music among the tribes of Indians in America.

In all styles of Indian music, the voice is the most important instrument.

To accompany the singing and dancing, Indians use drums and rattles.

Each drum and rattle has a design of its own.

Through these designs, the Indian shows his feeling for things in Nature.

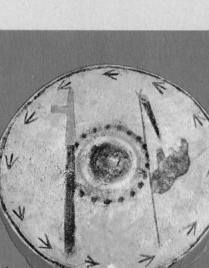

80

The singers follow a song leader, who sets the tempo and decides how high or how low they will sing.

Listen to the accompaniment of these Indian songs.
Which ones use rattles?
Which ones use drums?

◎ Navajo Night Chant
4
◎ Sioux Rabbit Dance
4
◎ Stomp Dance
4

You heard a special way of singing and playing found in much Indian music.
When you listen again, notice some other things to be found in the music of American Indians.

1. Much repetition of melodies and rhythm patterns
2. Very little or no harmony
3. Simple or no accompaniment
4. Tone colors of percussion instruments

Style: American Indian 81

OH, WHAT A BEAUTIFUL CITY

BLACK SPIRITUAL

A REFRAIN

Oh, what a beau - ti - ful cit - y,_____

Oh, what a beau - ti - ful cit - y,_____

Oh, what a beau - ti - ful cit - y, ___

Twelve gates - a to the cit - y, ___ Hal - le - lu - jah!

B VERSE

Three gates ___ to the East,

Three gates ___ to the West,

Three gates ___ to the North, ___

Three gates ___ to the South,

There's twelve gates - a to the cit - y, ___ Hal - le - lu - jah!

This song has two sections, A and B.

Listen for the accents in section B.

Clap hands on each accent.

A

B

Sometimes one section of music is different from another.

It is a *contrast*.

How is section B a *contrast* of section A in this song?

BOIL THEM CABBAGE DOWN
AMERICAN PIONEER SONG

FROM MORE SONGS OF THE NEW WORLD BY DESMOND MACMAHON, PUBLISHED BY HOLMES MCDOUGALL LIMITED

A VERSE

1. The rac-coon's got a fur-ry tail,

The pos-sum's tail is bare,—

The rab-bit ain't got no tail at all,

But a lit-tle bit o' bunch o' hair.

B REFRAIN

Boil them cab-bage down, down, Bake them bis-cuits brown, brown,

The on-ly tune I ev-er did learn is Boil them cab-bage down.

2. The June bug he has wings of gold,
   The firefly wings of flame,
   The bedbug's got no wings at all,
   But he gets there just the same. *Refrain*

3. Oh, love it is a killing fit
   When beauty hits a blossom,
   And if you want your finger bit,
   Just poke it at a possum. *Refrain*

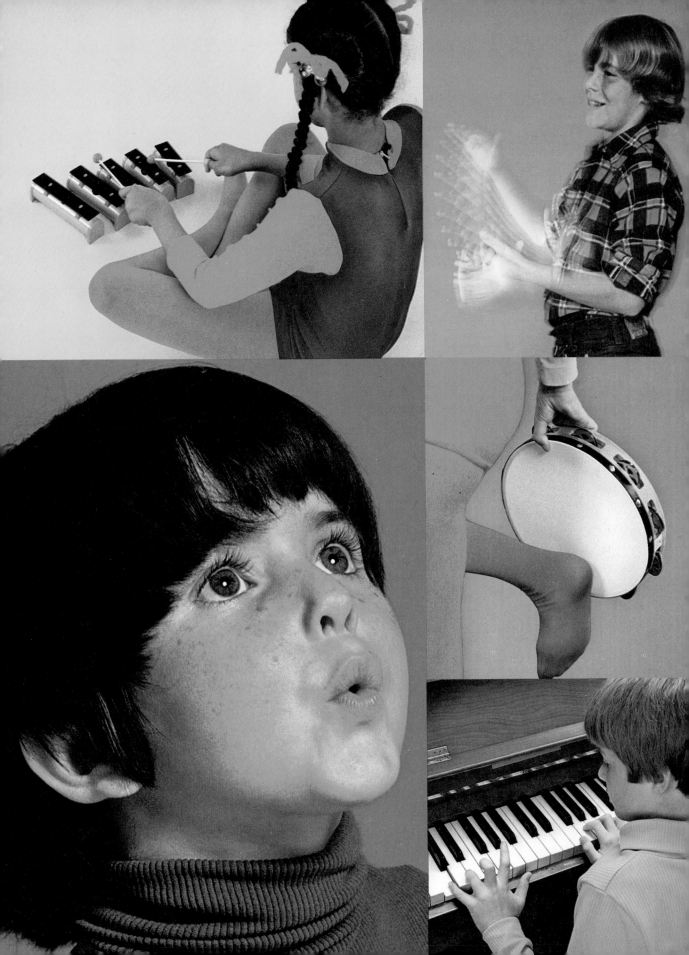

Add contrasting sections of your own to those on the recording.

Look at the directions for section A.

SOUND PIECE 3: Sound on Sound

DORIS HAYS

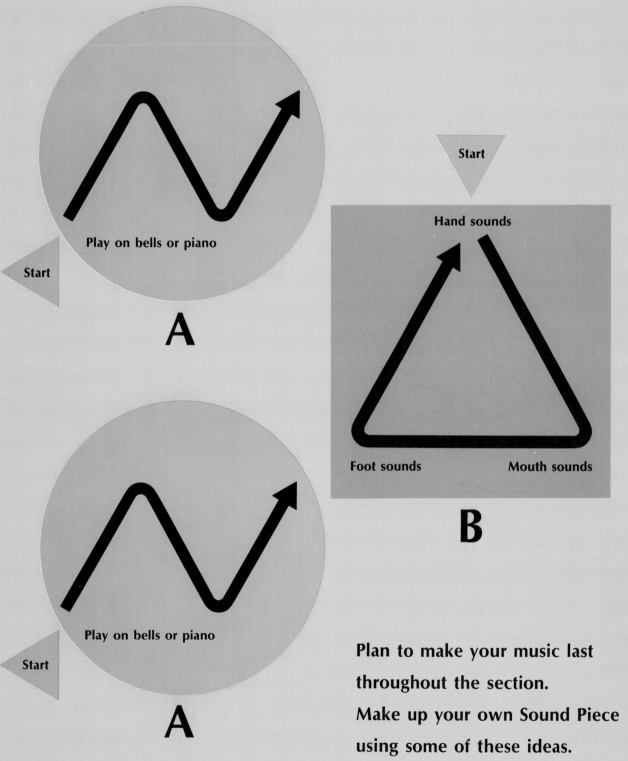

Play on bells or piano

Start

A

Start

Hand sounds

Foot sounds   Mouth sounds

B

Play on bells or piano

Start

A

Plan to make your music last throughout the section.

Make up your own Sound Piece using some of these ideas.

Which set of shapes and letters shows the form of "Little David, Play on Your Harp"?

AB
ABA

Follow the notes for each section as you sing the song.

LITTLE DAVID, PLAY ON YOUR HARP

BLACK SPIRITUAL

REFRAIN

Lit - tle Da - vid, play on your harp, Hal - le - lu, hal - le - lu,

Fine

Lit - tle Da - vid, play on your harp, Hal - le - lu.

VERSE

Lit - tle Da - vid was a shep-herd boy,_____

D.C. al Fine

He killed Go - li - ath and shout-ed for joy.

88 Form

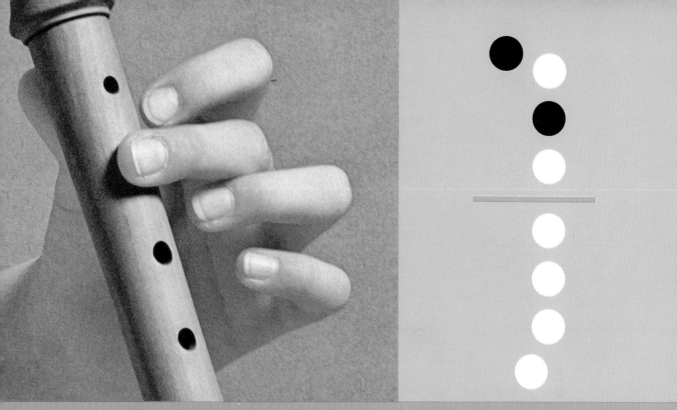

High C

Play one of these parts throughout section A of "Little David, Play on Your Harp."

1.

2.

Now try a countermelody for "Ain't Gonna Rain," page 24.

1.

2.

OH, WON'T YOU SIT DOWN?

BLACK SPIRITUAL

A REFRAIN

SOLO — CHORUS

Oh, won't you sit down?__ Lord, I can't sit down.__

SOLO — CHORUS

Oh, won't you sit down?__ Lord, I can't sit down.__

SOLO — CHORUS

Oh, won't you sit down?__ Lord, I can't sit down.__

Fine

'Cause I just got to Heav-en, gon-na look a-round.__

B VERSE

SOLO

1. Who's that yon-der dressed in red?__

Must be the chil-dren that__ Mo-ses led.__

Who's that yon-der dressed in white?__

Must be the chil-dren of the Is - rael - ite._____

2. Who's that yonder dressed in blue?

   Must be the children that are comin' through.

   Who's that yonder dressed in black?

   Must be the hypocrites a-turnin' back. *Refrain*

Can you hear and feel different sections in other music?

Look at the charts to help you.

CALL CHART 3: FORM ◉₄   CALL CHART 4: FORM ◉₄

1. *A*	**1.** *A*
2. *A (REPETITION)*	**2.** *A (REPETITION)*
3. *B (CONTRAST)*	**3.** *B (CONTRAST)*
4. *A (REPETITION)*	**4.** *B (CONTRAST)*

Tchaikovsky: "Trepak"   **Purcell:** *Trumpet Tune*

Make up a tambourine part for each section of this song.

Which section has meter in 3?

Which section has meter in 2?

PINATA SONG

CHRISTMAS SONG FROM MEXICO   ENGLISH WORDS BY VERNE MUNOZ

In the hap - py days   of Christ - mas, _____

Sounds of glad - ness fill   the   air; _____

When it's time   for the   pi - ña - ta, _____

There's ex - cite - ment ev - 'ry - where. __

Take a stick and whack it,   Be the one to crack it;

Win pi - ña - ta's trea - sure, Can - dies for your plea - sure.

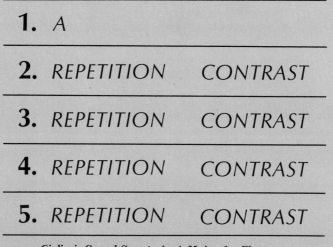

When the music starts and the voice on the recording says "one," you are hearing section A, as shown on the chart.

At each number that follows, decide whether the section is a *repetition* of A or a *contrast* of A.

1. *A*		
2. REPETITION		CONTRAST
3. REPETITION		CONTRAST
4. REPETITION		CONTRAST
5. REPETITION		CONTRAST

Giuliani: *Grand Sonata in A Major for Flute and Guitar*, "Scherzo" (excerpt)

1. *A*		
2. REPETITION		CONTRAST
3. REPETITION		CONTRAST
4. REPETITION		CONTRAST

Pinto: "Run Run"

Look around your classroom.

What can you find that repeats?

What can you find that contrasts?

Can you find repetition and contrast in this painting?

Can you find repetition and contrast in this poem?

BUT YOU ARE MINE ◎
5

Someone would like to have you for her child
but you are mine.
Someone would like to rear you on a costly mat
but you are mine.
Someone would like to place you on a camel blanket
but you are mine.

I have you to rear on a torn old mat.

Someone would like to have you as her child

but you are mine.

—From Africa

Now say the poem to find the ideas that contrast.

There is repetition and contrast in music and painting and poetry.

Each art uses repetition and contrast in its own way.

Sound is made by a kind of motion
called *vibration*—movement
back and forth.

Experiment with vibration by
striking, blowing, or plucking
to discover differences
in sound.

Some sounds are high.

Some sounds are low.

Which sounds higher?

Which sounds higher?

Why?

Which sounds higher?

Why?

Which sounds higher?

Why?

THE SOW TOOK THE MEASLES

AMERICAN FRONTIER SONG

How do you think I be - gan in the world?

I got me a sow and sev - 'ral oth - er thing.

The sow took the mea - sles and she died in the spring.

1. What do you think I made of her hide?

The ver - y best sad - dle that you ev - er did ride.

Sad - dle or bri - dle or an - y such thing,

D.C. after verse 4

The sow took the mea - sles and she died in the spring.

2. What do you think I made of her nose?

The very best thimble that ever sewed clothes.

Thimble or thread or any such thing,

The sow took the measles and she died in the spring.

3. What do you think I made of her tail?

   The very best whup that ever sought sail.

   Whup or whupsocket or any such thing,

   The sow took the measles and she died in the spring.

4. What do you think I made of her feet?

   The very best pickles that you ever did eat.

   Pickles or glue or any such thing,

   The sow took the measles and she died in the spring. *Refrain*

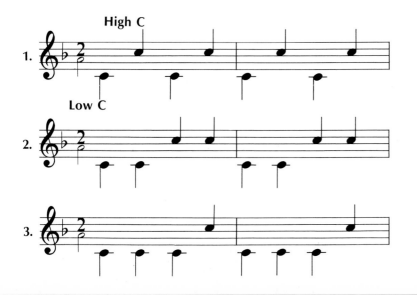

The Call Chart will help you hear when the music is mostly low, mostly high, and both low and high.

CALL CHART 5: REGISTER

1. *MOSTLY LOW*

2. *MOSTLY HIGH*

3. *BOTH LOW AND HIGH*

4. *MOSTLY LOW*

Mussorgsky: *Pictures at an Exhibition,* "Samuel Goldenberg and Schmuyle"

Find a space in the room to walk a low-high-high pattern.

How can you show low steps? high steps?

While some children move, take turns playing one of the

instruments to accompany them.

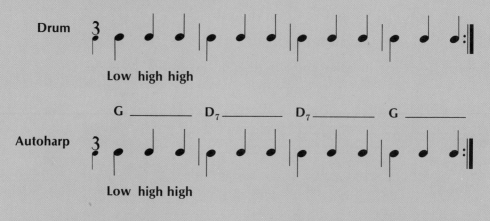

Drum

Low high high

Autoharp

Low high high

Low D

To play a recorder part for

"Bella Bimba," you need

a new note, high D.

High D

Add your accompaniment to section A of this song.

Stop and listen to section B.

BELLA BIMBA

FOLK SONG FROM ITALY   ENGLISH WORDS BY RICHARD MORRIS

2. Whirling and twirling,

   Round and around,

   Feet always moving

   When music sounds.

You have played high and low sounds on a drum, on the strings of an Autoharp, or on a recorder.

Now play a bell part to accompany section A of "Bella Bimba."

Call the lower note "one" and count all the lines and spaces to the higher note. It will be "eight." The two notes are an *octave* apart.

Now play the notes, *octave* D, at the same time to discover that they sound alike.

Find other bells that sound the same when played together.

Your ears will tell you when you are playing octaves.

Play octaves to accompany "Bella Bimba."

Play octave D during section A.

Play octave B during section B.

Make up your own rhythm pattern.

WHAT DO YOU HEAR? 6: REGISTER ◉5

Each time a number is called, decide whether the music is mostly high or mostly low.

If you think it is mostly high, circle the words MOSTLY HIGH. If you think it is mostly low, circle the words MOSTLY LOW. Listen. Then circle what you hear.

1	*MOSTLY HIGH*	*MOSTLY LOW*
2	*MOSTLY HIGH*	*MOSTLY LOW*
3	*MOSTLY HIGH*	*MOSTLY LOW*
4	*MOSTLY HIGH*	*MOSTLY LOW*
5	*MOSTLY HIGH*	*MOSTLY LOW*
6	*MOSTLY HIGH*	*MOSTLY LOW*

Haydn: *Symphony No. 103,* "Adagio"

1	*MOSTLY HIGH*	*MOSTLY LOW*
2	*MOSTLY HIGH*	*MOSTLY LOW*
3	*MOSTLY HIGH*	*MOSTLY LOW*

Grieg: "In the Hall of the Mountain King"
Beethoven: *Symphony No. 7,* Movement 4
Britten: *The Young Person's Guide to the Orchestra*

ONE DAY MY MOTHER WENT TO THE MARKET

FOLK SONG FROM ITALY   ENGLISH WORDS BY LEO ISRAEL   COLLECTED AND ADAPTED BY RUDOLPH GOEHR

Oh, he said, "Cock - a doo - dle - doo,"

And a - way he flew, and a - way he flew.

2. . . . and she bought a little pig . . .

But when my mother started to cook him,

He got up and danced a jig . . .

Oh, he said, "Oink, oink, oink,

Though I'd like to stay, though I'd like to stay."

Oh, he said, "Oink, oink, oink,"

And he ran away, and he ran away.

3. . . . and she bought a pretty lamb . . .

But when my mother started to cook him,

He said, "Who do you think I am?" . . .

Oh, he said, "Baa, baa, baa,

I'm silly, it's true, I'm silly, it's true."

Oh, he said, "Baa, baa, baa,

Not as silly as you, not as silly as you."

4. . . . and she bought a lovely hen . . .

But when my mother started to cook her,

She began to cluck again . . .

Oh, she said, "Cluck, cluck, cluck, cluck, cluck."

But she forgot, but she forgot,

Oh, she said, "Cluck, cluck, cluck, cluck, cluck,"

And fell into the pot, and fell into the pot.

Tempo, dynamics, beat, direction, register,
and tone color are some of the *qualities* of music.

They can be put together in different ways to make different *styles*.
As you listen to two pieces in different styles, look at the symbols
to find some of the qualities you hear.
Each piece has a different style, or general sound.

🔆 Locke: Courante   🔆 Brahms: Hungarian Dance No. 6

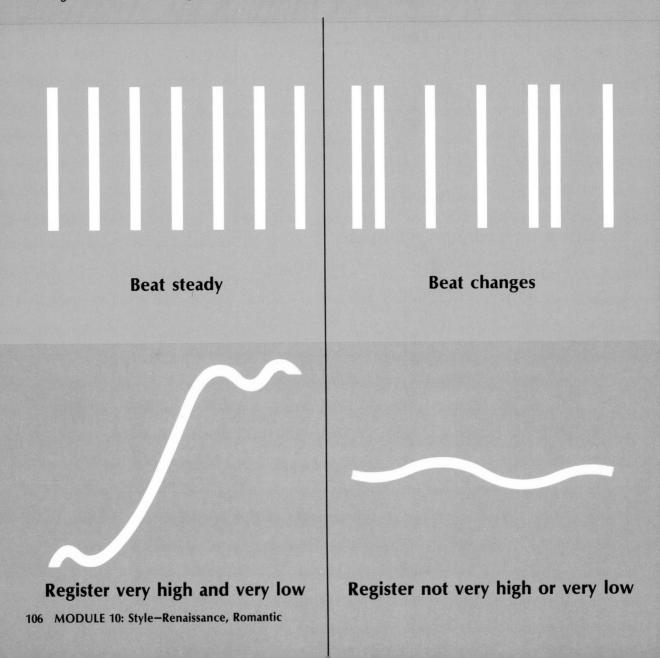

Beat steady   Beat changes

Register very high and very low   Register not very high or very low

Small group of instruments

Large group of instruments

Accents

No accents

Few dynamic changes

Many dynamic changes

Words can have short
sounds or long sounds.
Listen to this poem.
Which sound is the
longest on the recording?

BLUM

Dog means dog,

And cat means cat;

And there are lots

Of words like that.

A cart's a cart

To pull or shove,

A plate's a plate,

To eat off of.

But there are other

Words I say

When I am left

Alone to play.

Blum is one.

Blum is a word

That very few

Have ever heard.

I like to say it.

"Blum, Blum, Blum"—

I do it loud

Or in a hum.

All by itself

It's nice to sing:

It does not mean

A single thing.

Dorothy Aldis

Music can have long and short sounds, too.

Which sounds are short and which are long in this song?

WHAT IS LOVE?

WORDS AND MUSIC BY CHRIS DEDRICK © 1972 ALMITRA MUSIC COMPANY, INC.

I know a ver - y hard ques - tion: What is love?

Ver - y wise peo - ple can't find the words to say what love is.

I fig-ured out that there can't be words for some-thing quite that good.

If you stop, If you stop to think a - bout your friends, your folks,

Your pup - py, your cat, the sun - shine, the trees and e - ven your - self—

You know all a - bout love; Al - most ev - 'ry - one does.

Love, love, I know all a - bout love, but I can't tell.

Love, love, Words can't tell a - bout love, it's just as well.

Do you *see* what you *hear*?

Sing the song and point to the longest sounds.

109

HOW TO WRITE LONG AND SHORT SOUNDS
Find these notes in the song "Love" on page 109.

Quarter notes

Half notes

Whole notes

Eighth notes

How many quarter notes can take the place of a half note?

How many eighth notes can take the place of a half note?

How many eighth notes can take the place of a quarter note?

How many quarter notes can take the place of a whole note?

Long and short sounds can make a rhythm pattern.

Find these patterns in the music on page 109.

Play this pattern when it comes in the song "Love."

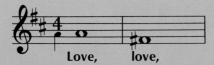

Can you hear long and short sounds in a piano piece?

Listen to the recording and check the chart to help you.

CALL CHART 6: DURATION

Chopin: *Scherzo No. 3 in C♯ Minor*

1. *LONG SOUNDS*	4. *SHORT SOUNDS*
2. *SHORT SOUNDS*	5. *LONG SOUNDS*
3. *LONG SOUNDS*	6. *SHORT SOUNDS*
	7. *LONG SOUNDS*

Clap a pattern of shorter sounds each time you hear a long sound in this song.

OLD BLUE SOUTHERN MOUNTAIN SONG

1. I had an old dog,_____

And his name was Blue,_____

And I bet-cha five dol-lars he's a good dog, too.

REFRAIN

Come on, Blue,_____ you good dog,__ you;_____

Come on, Blue,_____ you good dog,__ you.

2. I grabbed my axe and I tooted my horn,
   Gonna git me a 'possum in the new-ground corn. *Refrain*

3. Chased that ol' 'possum up a 'simmon tree,
   Blue looked at the 'possum, 'possum looked at me. *Refrain*

4. Blue grinned at me, I grinned at him,
   I shook out the 'possum, Blue took him in. *Refrain*

5. Baked that 'possum all good and brown,
   And I laid them sweet potatoes 'round and 'round. *Refrain*

6. Well, old Blue died, and he died so hard,
   That he shook the ground in my back yard. *Refrain*

7. I dug his grave with a silver spade,
   I let him down with a golden chain. *Refrain*

8. When I get to heaven, first thing I'll do,
   Grab me a horn and blow for old Blue. *Refrain*

Can you hear two different rhythm patterns played at the same time in this music?

Vivaldi: *The Four Seasons* (Winter)

Baldridge: *Let's Dance*

THE PIG

FOLK TUNE FROM MEXICO   ENGLISH WORDS BY MARGARET MARKS

Mis - sus Tor - res had a pi - hig,

Ver - y fat and ver - y bi - hig,

Dressed him in a fun - ny wi - hig,

Tried to make him dance a ji - hig.

But the pig, whose name was Sa - ham,

Said, "I'm ver - y sor - ry, Ma - ham,

Can't you leave me as I a - ham?

I don't want to be a ha - ham!"

AFRICAN RHYTHM COMPLEX

Chant the numbers in each line. Clap each time you say a large-size number.

1 2 3 4 5 6 7 8 9 10 11 12

1 2 3 4 5 6 7 8 9 10 11 12

1 2 3 4 5 6 7 8 9 10 11 12

Look at the notation for the rhythms you clapped.

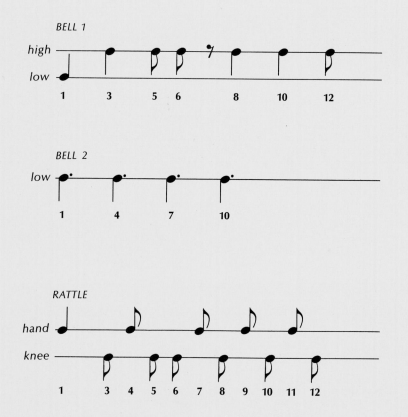

BELL 1
high
low
1   3   5   6   8   10   12

BELL 2
low
1   4   7   10

RATTLE
hand
knee
1   3   4   5   6   7   8   9   10   11   12

Sound and silence can work together in a rhythm pattern.

SCRATCH, SCRATCH

WORDS AND MUSIC BY HARRY BELAFONTE AND LORD BURGESS

1. Oh, we went out to a par - ty,

It was me and Ben and Mac,

And be - fore I knew what hap - pened,

I got an itch - in' on my back.

REFRAIN

Scratch, scratch me back, Scratch, scratch me back.

It real - ly is a fact,____

The less I itch, the more I scratch.

2. Well, I was quite embarrassed,
   Till my two friends I did see,
   Well, they were madly itching,
   And they were screaming louder than me.
   Refrain

3. Now, this scratching was contagious,
   And it didn't take very long,
   Ev'rybody there was itching,
   As they joined me in this song.
   Refrain

Keep time to the steady beat as you say this patting chant.
Notice how sound and silence work together.

RABBIT HASH PATTING CHANT

Collected, adapted and arranged by John A. Lomax & Alan Lomax   TRO—© Copyright 1934 and renewed 1962 Ludlow Music, Inc., New York, N.Y. Used by permission

Oh, rab - bit, rab - bit, rab - bit, rab - bit a - hash,

An' pole - cat smash.

Rab - bit, rab - bit, rab - bit a - hash.

Rab - bit skip, an' rab - bit hop, An' rab - bit eat my tur - nip top.

Oh, rab - bit, rab - bit, rab - bit a - hash!

Oh, rab - bit a - hash!

Tap out the rhythm pattern of the melody to hear the rhythm patterns that repeat.

THE BARNYARD

WORDS AND MUSIC BY CARMINO RAVOSA

© 1972 Carmino Ravosa

1. Barn - yard, barn - yard, all a-round the barn - yard,

Hear the cow go, "Moo, moo."

Barn - yard, barn - yard, all a-round the barn - yard,

Hear the duck go, "Quack, quack."

All a-round the barn-yard, An - i - mals are talk - ing;

Though it sounds to you like Just a lot of squawk-ing.

Barn - yard, barn - yard, all a-round the barn - yard,

Hear the goose go, "Honk, honk."

Barn - yard, barn - yard, all a-round the barn - yard,

Hear the chick-en, "Cluck, cluck, Cluck, cluck."

2. Barnyard, barnyard, all around the barnyard,

Hear the pig go, "Oink, oink."

Barnyard, barnyard, all around the barnyard,

Hear the sheep go, "Baa, baa."

All around the barnyard,

Animals are talking;

Though it sounds to you like

Just a lot of squawking.

Barnyard, barnyard, all around the barnyard,

Hear the horse go, "Neigh, neigh."

Barnyard, barnyard, all around the barnyard,

Hear the donkey, "Hee-haw, Hee-haw."

Bartók: *Roumanian Dance No. 6*

In music, a sudden loud sound is called an *accent.*

Find the sign (>) that shows accent in this song.

SHEPHERDS CAME TO BETHLEHEM POLISH CAROL

ENGLISH WORDS BY ROSEMARY JACQUES

1. Shep-herds came to Beth - le - hem on Christ - mas Day.

How the Ba - by smiled as they their pipes did play.

Glo - ry, sing glo - ry to God in the high - est,

And peace on earth, Peace on earth.

2. Then a shepherd beat upon a little drum.
   How it pleased the Baby with its rum-tum-tum.
   Glory, . . .

3. As the shepherds bowed before the blessed Boy,
   All the heavens rang with sounds of wondrous joy.
   Glory, . . .

Play the accents on a small drum or on finger cymbals.

To accompany "Shepherds Came to Bethlehem," play one of the parts on the bells or recorder.

Here is a part to play on a tambourine.

WHAT DO YOU HEAR? 7: DURATION

What do you hear? Each time a number is called, decide whether you hear mostly short sounds, mostly long sounds, or short and long sounds played together.

Listen. Then circle what you hear.

---

1. SHORT SOUNDS
LONG SOUNDS
SHORT AND LONG SOUNDS PLAYED TOGETHER

---

2 SHORT SOUNDS
LONG SOUNDS
SHORT AND LONG SOUNDS PLAYED TOGETHER

---

3 SHORT SOUNDS
LONG SOUNDS
SHORT AND LONG SOUNDS PLAYED TOGETHER

---

4 SHORT SOUNDS
LONG SOUNDS
SHORT AND LONG SOUNDS PLAYED TOGETHER

Hays: *Sound Piece 3*
Vivaldi: *The Four Seasons* (Winter)
Ebreo: *Falla con misuras*
Mama Paquita

What do you hear? As each number is called, look at the notation and circle the rhythm pattern you hear.

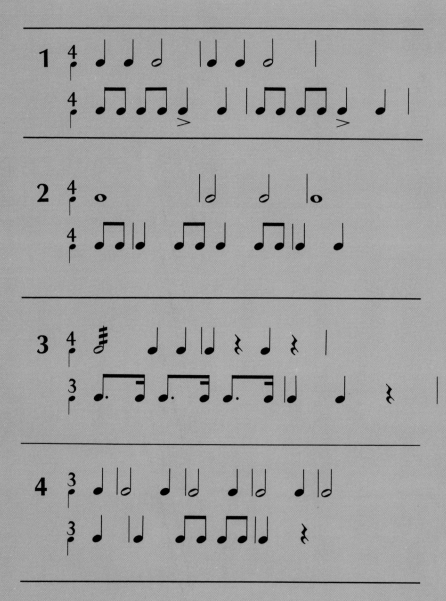

The Lilly Bud
Mozart: *Symphony No. 40*
The Pig
Bach: *Passacaglia in C Minor*

You can use your voice to make different tone colors.

Find words that imitate sounds in this poem.

When you say the poem, make your voice imitate the sounds.

LEWIS HAS A TRUMPET

A trumpet
A trumpet
Lewis has a trumpet
A bright one that's yellow
A loud proud horn.
He blows it in the evening
When the moon is newly rising
He blows it when it's raining
In the cold and misty morn
It honks and it whistles
It roars like a lion
It rumbles like a lion
With a wheezy huffing hum
His parents say it's awful
Oh really simply awful
But
Lewis says he loves it
It's such a handsome trumpet
And when he's through with trumpets
He's going to buy a drum.

Karla Kuskin

Whistles honks wheezy ROAR Huffing HUM Rumbles

The recorder has its own tone color.
When you play a recorder, you make
the sound by blowing.
All instruments that are played by
blowing are called *wind instruments*.
How many do you know?

French horn

clarinet

recorder

trumpet and trombone

flute

Do you know
wind instruments
by their tone color?
Point to the picture
that shows what
you hear on the recording.

Tone Colors of Wind Instruments

Here are some songs to play on the recorder.

HANA ICHI MOMME
FOLK SONG FROM JAPAN

Ka - te u - re - shii___ ha - na i - chi mom - me.

Mu - ka - i no da - re ka san chot - to o - i - de.

Add the tone color of the woodblock when it comes in the song.

Add one of these parts to the melody.

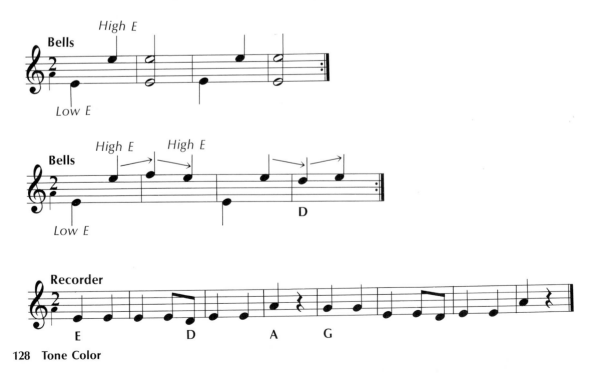

IMAGINATION OF GRAND SEA

FOLK SONG FROM JAPAN

ENGLISH WORDS BY RICHARD MORRIS

U - mi wa hi - ro - i na oh - ki - i na,

Tsu - ki ga no - bo - ru shi hi ga shi - zu - mu.

1. *Grand is the evening sea, majestic and deep;*

   There, as the moon awakes, the sun will go to sleep.

2. *Calm are the mighty waves; the water, so blue;*

   I wonder where the sea and all the waves go to.

3. *Many the tiny ships that float on the sea;*

   Some day to foreign lands those ships will carry me.

AY, DI, DI, DI

HASIDIC MELODY

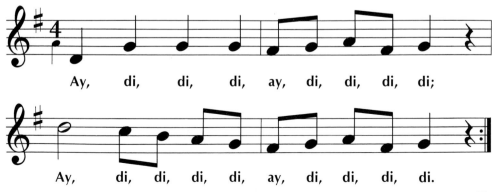

Ay, di, di, di, ay, di, di, di, di;

Ay, di, di, di, di, ay, di, di, di, di.

YANKEE DOODLE

TRADITIONAL   WORDS BY DR. RICHARD SHUCKBURGH

1. 7 Fath'r and I went down to camp,
2. And there we saw a thou - sand men,

A - long with Cap - tain Good - in',
As rich as Squire____ Da - vid;

And there we saw the men and boys
And what they wast - ed ev - 'ry day,

As thick as hast y pud - din'.
I wish it could be sav - ed.

REFRAIN

Yan - kee Doo - dle, keep it up, Yan - kee Doo - dle dan - dy,

Mind the mu - sic and the step And with the girls be hand - y.

3. And there was Captain Washington

Upon a slapping stallion,

A-giving orders to his men;

I guess there was a million.   Drum

Cymbals

BATTLE HYMN OF THE REPUBLIC

MUSIC BY WILLIAM STEFFE

WORDS BY JULIA WARD HOWE

Glo - ry, glo - ry, hal - le - lu - jah!

Glo - ry, glo - ry, hal - le - lu - jah!

Glo - ry, glo - ry, hal - le - lu - jah! His truth is march-ing on.

Drum

Cymbals

JINGLE BELLS

WORDS AND MUSIC BY JAMES PIERPONT

Jin - gle bells, jin - gle bells, jin - gle all the way!

Oh, what fun it is to ride in a one-horse o - pen sleigh!

Jin - gle bells, jin - gle bells, jin - gle all the way!

Oh, what fun it is to ride in a one-horse o - pen sleigh!

You can add the tone color of the Autoharp when
you sing these songs.

FOR HEALTH AND STRENGTH

OLD ENGLISH ROUND

For health and strength and dai - ly food We praise Thy name, O Lord.

FRERE JACQUES

FRENCH ROUND

Frè - re Jac - ques, Frè - re Jac - ques,

Dor - mez - vous, Dor - mez - vous?

Son - nez les ma - ti - nes, Son - nez les ma - ti - nes,

Din din don, Din din don.

OH, SUSANNA

WORDS AND MUSIC BY STEPHEN FOSTER

I came from Al - a - ba - ma With my ban - jo on my knee,

I'm going to Loui - si - an - a, My true love for to see;

It rained all night the day I left, The weath - er it was dry;

The sun so hot I froze to death; Su - san - na, don't you cry.

REFRAIN

Oh, Su - san - na, Oh, don't you cry for me,

I've come from Al - a - ba - ma With my ban - jo on my knee.

2. I had a dream the other night,

When ev'rything was still.

I thought I saw Susanna

A-coming down the hill.

The buckwheat cake was in her mouth,

The tear was in her eye.

Says I, "I'm coming from the South,

Susanna, don't you cry." *Refrain*

Tone Color 133

NOBODY'S BUSINESS

AMERICAN FOLK SONG

FROM PLAY-PARTY GAMES OF PIONEER TIMES, PUBLISHED BY COOPERATIVE RECREATION SERVICE, INC. USED BY PERMISSION.

VERSE

1. I went to town in a lit-tle red wag-on,

Come back home with the hub a-drag-gin',

It's no-bod-y's busi-ness what I do.

REFRAIN

It's no-bod-y's busi-ness, busi-ness,

No-bod-y's busi-ness, busi-ness,

No-bod-y's busi-ness what I do.

2. I've got a wife and she's a daisy,

   She won't work and I'm too lazy,

   It's nobody's business what I do. *Refrain*

Add the tone color of one of the parts on page 135 as others sing this song.

134 Tone Color

Which part will you play?

This part uses B A G only.

This part uses B A G, low D, and F#.

Vivaldi: *The Four Seasons* (Winter)

6

Listen for the bell part in this song.

Do you see it in section A, or in section B? Section B

GERMAN INSTRUMENT SONG

FOLK SONG FROM GERMANY

ENGLISH WORDS BY TULLA STATLER

1. If I had a bell to play a tune on,

   If I had a bell, oh, how I'd *ring.*

Instrumental Part (Bells)

B   A   G   F#

2. If I had a fiddle, fiddle, fiddle,

   If I had a fiddle, how I'd *bow.*

3. If I had a pipe to play a tune on,

   If I had a pipe, oh, how I'd *blow.*

4. If I had an Autoharp to play on,

   If I had an Autoharp, I'd *strum.*

5. If I had a drum that I could play on,

   If I had a drum, oh, how I'd *beat.*

6. Now we have a tune to play together,

   Now we have a tune, oh, how we'll *play.*

Add the tone color of other instruments to the bell part in "German Instrument Song."

When the instruments play together, you hear *harmony*.

CALL CHART 7: TONE COLOR

Some musical sounds are made by voices.

Others are made by instruments.

When a number is called, look at the pictures

to discover how the sound is made.

Match the sounds with the pictures.

1. The *dulcimer* is strummed, plucked, or struck with mallets.

2. The *bass drum* is struck.

3. To play the *organ*, the player strikes the keys;
   a machine blows air across and through the pipes.

4. In an electronic laboratory, electric machines make sounds.

5. The player strikes the keys of the *piano*.
   Hammers then strike the strings. Sometimes the player may
   strike, pluck, or strum the strings without using the keys.

6. The *bassoon* is played by blowing.

7. The *timpani* are struck with mallets.

8. A *guitar* can be strummed or plucked.
   Sometimes the player strikes the body of the guitar.

Old Bald Eagle
Ibert: "Parade"
Mozart: *Adagio and Fugue in C Minor*
Ussachevsky: *Four Miniatures No. 1*

Ibert: "Le Water-Chute"
Nielson: *Quintet Op. 43*
Rooker: *Horn in the West,* "Drum Theme"
McHugh: *Vegetables II*

FORTY-NINE ANGELS

WORDS AND MUSIC BY ROBERT SCHMERTZ

FROM A PICTURE BOOK OF SONGS AND BALLADS BY ROBERT SCHMERTZ. USED BY PERMISSION.

Forty-nine angels looking down, Seven all around a golden crown,
Forty-nine angels looking down, Seven weaving linen for a gown,

Seven with a harp and seven with a horn Play for the Baby
Seven to embroider, seven to adorn A dress for the Baby

newly born, Play for the Baby newly born.
newly born, A dress for the Baby newly born.

And where are the rest of the forty-nine? One takes a star, makes it

brightly shine; Two tell the news over Galilee;

Three show the way to the Wise Men three; And little Forty-Nine this

blessed morn Sings for the Baby newly born,

Sings for the Baby newly born.

When each number is called, decide what tone color you hear.

Listen. Then circle your answer.

1	*TRUMPET AND TROMBONE*	*FLUTE*	*CLARINET*	*AUTOHARP*
2	*TRUMPET AND TROMBONE*	*FLUTE*	*CLARINET*	*AUTOHARP*
3	*TRUMPET AND TROMBONE*	*FLUTE*	*CLARINET*	*AUTOHARP*
4	*TRUMPET AND TROMBONE*	*FLUTE*	*CLARINET*	*AUTOHARP*
5	*TRUMPET AND TROMBONE*	*FLUTE*	*CLARINET*	*AUTOHARP*

Debussy: *Syrinx*
Mozart: *Concerto for Clarinet and Orchestra,* K. 622, "Adagio"
Eddleman: *Autoharp Sound Piece*
Gabrieli: *Canzona Noni Toni*
Messiaen: *Abyss of the Birds*

Music has styles, too.

**How many of these things
can you hear
in a piece in *classic style*?**

🎵 Mozart: *Horn Concerto in E♭*

1 STEADY BEAT

2 BEATS MOVING
  IN TWOS

3 LONG AND SHORT
  PHRASES

4 TONAL
  (FOCUSES ON THE
  IMPORTANT TONE)

5 MELODY
  WITH HARMONY

6 TONE COLOR:
  FRENCH HORN AND
  ORCHESTRA

Listen to another piece.

**Do you think it is
in the same style,
or does it sound different?**

🎵 Phillips: *California Dreamin'*

1 STEADY BEAT

2 BEATS MOVING
  IN TWOS

3 LONG AND SHORT
  PHRASES

4 TONAL
  (FOCUSES ON ONE
  IMPORTANT TONE)

5 MELODY
  WITH HARMONY

6 TONE COLOR:
  BASS GUITAR, DRUMS,
  TRUMPETS, ORGAN, VOICES

**Just as cars in different styles can have some of the same parts,
pieces of music in different styles can have some of the same parts.**

The same parts can create a different look or sound, called *style*.

Music has long and short phrases. Follow the long and short phrase lines as you listen to this song.

HOW D'YE DO AND SHAKE HANDS

MUSIC BY OLIVER WALLACE

WORDS BY CY COBEN

© 1951 WALT DISNEY MUSIC COMPANY. REPRINTED BY PERMISSION.

You go through life and nev - er know the day when fate may bring

A sit - u - a - tion that will prove to be em - bar - rass - ing.

Your face gets red, you hide your head, and wish that you could die,____

But that's old - fash - ioned, here's a new thing you should real - ly try.

Say "How d' ye do" and shake hands, Shake hands, shake hands,

Say "How d' ye do" and shake hands, State your name and bus' - ness.

Sing from here to the end four times.

Music has phrases. Poems have phrases, too.

PAPER I

Paper is two kinds, to write on, to wrap with.

If you like to write, you write.

If you like to wrap, you wrap.

Some papers like writers, some like wrappers.

Are you a writer or a wrapper?

Carl Sandburg

APRIL FOOL'S DAY

Look out! Look out! You've spilt the ink.

You're sitting in a purple puddle.

Your pants are ripped and I should think

You'd hate to have a nose so pink

And hair in such a dreadful muddle.

Look out! Behind you there's a rat.

He's hiding now behind the stool.

He's going to jump upon your hat.

Look out! Watch out! Oh dear, what's THAT?

It's only you, you April fool!

Marnie Pomeroy

HAWAIIAN RAINBOWS

HAWAIIAN FOLK SONG

Ha - wai - ian rain - bows, white clouds roll by;

You show your col - ors a - gainst the sky.

Ha - wai - ian rain - bows, it seems to me,

Reach from the moun - tain down to the sea.

YOU CAN'T MAKE A TURTLE COME OUT

WORDS AND MUSIC BY MALVINA REYNOLDS   © COPYRIGHT 1962 BY SCHRODER MUSIC CO. (ASCAP) USED BY PERMISSION.

1. You can't make a tur - tle come out,

You can't make a tur - tle come out,

You can call him or coax him or shake him or shout,

But you can't make a tur - tle come out, come out,

You can't make a tur - tle come out.

2. If he wants to stay in his shell, (*2 times*)

   You can knock on the door but you can't ring the bell,

   And you can't make a turtle come out, come out,

   You can't make a turtle come out.

3. Be kind to your four-footed friends, (*2 times*)

   A poke makes a turtle retreat at both ends,

   And you can't make a turtle come out, come out,

   You can't make a turtle come out.

4. So you'll have to patiently wait, (*2 times*)

   And when he gets ready he'll open the gate,

   But you can't make a turtle come out, come out,

   You can't make a turtle come out.

5. And when you forget that he's there, (*2 times*)

   He'll be walking around with his head in the air,

   But you can't make a turtle come out, come out,

   You can't make a turtle come out.

Make up your own phrase of sound by following one
of the parts below.
Make the phrase as long or as
short as you wish.

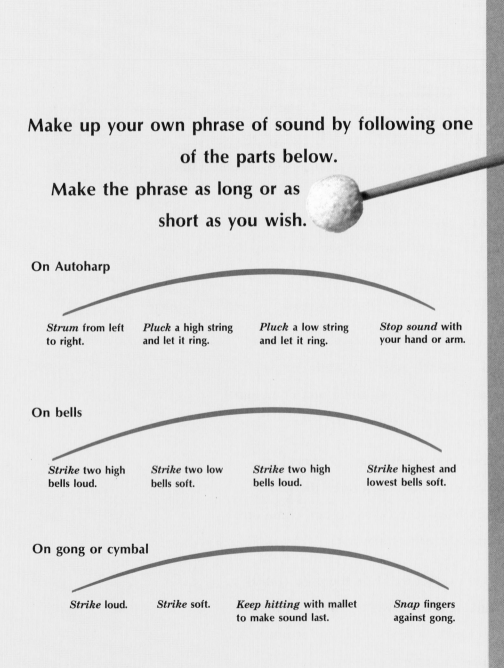

On Autoharp

Strum from left to right.

Pluck a high string and let it ring.

Pluck a low string and let it ring.

Stop sound with your hand or arm.

On bells

Strike two high bells loud.

Strike two low bells soft.

Strike two high bells loud.

Strike highest and lowest bells soft.

On gong or cymbal

Strike loud.

Strike soft.

Keep hitting with mallet to make sound last.

Snap fingers against gong.

To play
a phrase
of silence,
pretend to play
the instrument
without
making
a sound.

You have played a phrase of *sound* on the Autoharp, bells, gong, or cymbal.

Show a phrase of silence by pretending to play.

Now put the phrases together in ABA form.

SOUND PIECE 4: Sound and Silent Motion ELIZABETH CROOK

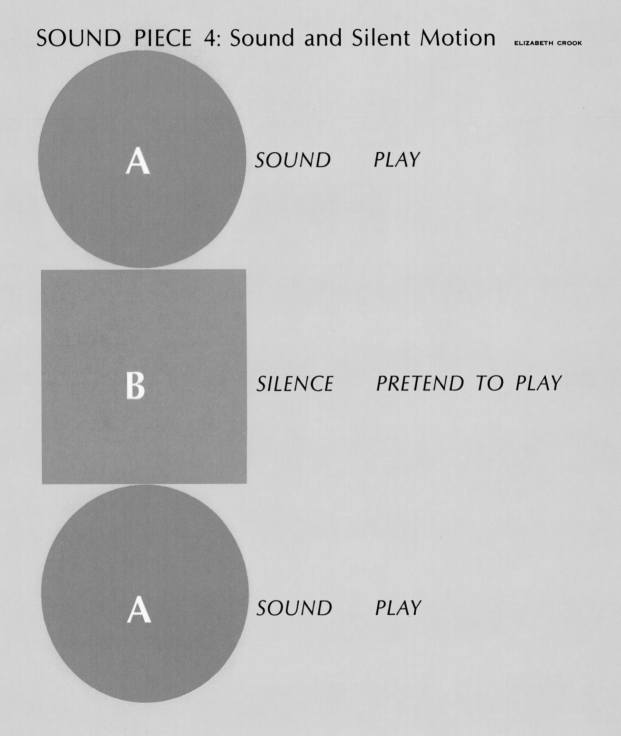

A   *SOUND*   *PLAY*

B   *SILENCE*   *PRETEND TO PLAY*

A   *SOUND*   *PLAY*

Can you feel the length of the phrases in songs you know?

Listen for the number of phrases in each song.

Then look at the chart to see if you are right.

CALL CHART 8: PHRASES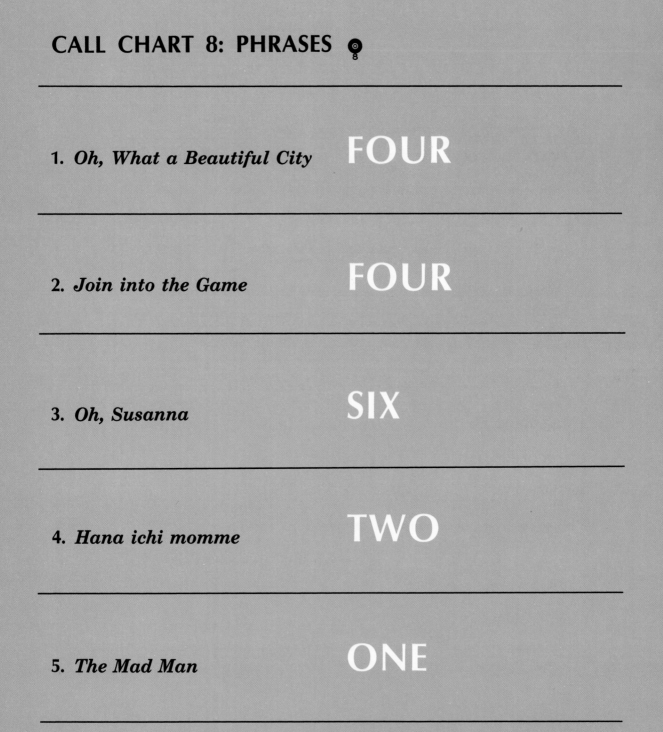

1. *Oh, What a Beautiful City*   FOUR

2. *Join into the Game*   FOUR

3. *Oh, Susanna*   SIX

4. *Hana ichi momme*   TWO

5. *The Mad Man*   ONE

Follow the notes to help you see and hear which phrase ends with a strong cadence.

JOYOUS CHANUKAH

HEBREW FOLK SONG   ENGLISH WORDS BY PHYLLIS RESNICK

Cha - nu - kah, Cha - nu - kah, hol - i - day so fair,

Glow - ing light, can - dles bright, hap - pi - ness we share.

Gai - ly dance, gai - ly sing while the drey - dl whirls,

Round and round, round and round, see how fast it twirls.

To accompany "Joyous Chanukah," add a tambourine or recorder part.

Tambourine

Shake

Play 4 times

Play steady beats.

Recorder or Bells

Play the rhythm of the words.

DEBKA HORA

FOLK SONG FROM ISRAEL

USED BY PERMISSION OF © LAWSON-GOULD MUSIC PUBLISHERS, INC.

La la la la la la la la, (clap)

La la la la la la la la. (clap)

La la la la la la la la la la,

La la la la la la la la. (clap)

SHEPHERDS BRING CANDY AND MILK

17TH-CENTURY CHRISTMAS SONG FROM BELGIUM   ENGLISH WORDS BY SALLI TERRI
FROM BELGIAN CHRISTMAS SONGS, SET I © 1971 BY LAWSON-GOULD MUSIC PUBLISHERS, INC. USED BY PERMISSION

Shep-herds, bring can - dy and milk to the Child.

See lit - tle Je - sus cry - ing there.

Hang up your coats to keep out the wind.

Jo - seph is rock - ing the Ba - by so mild.

2. Mary and angels are singing a song,

There in the stable shabby and bare.

Joseph so weary comes from the stream.

He washed the swaddling clothes all the day long.

3. Mary and Jesus are lying there.

Joseph is gath'ring wood for the fire.

See how he tends to all of the chores.

He loves the Baby and Mary fair.

WHAT DO YOU HEAR? 10: PHRASES (CADENCE)

Can you hear strong and weak cadences in music?
Decide whether the phrase ends with a strong cadence or
a weak cadence. Listen, then circle your answer.

1	STRONG	WEAK
2	STRONG	WEAK
3	STRONG	WEAK
4	STRONG	WEAK

Join into the Game

1	STRONG	WEAK
2	STRONG	WEAK
3	STRONG	WEAK
4	STRONG	WEAK
5	STRONG	WEAK
6	STRONG	WEAK

Oh, Susanna

Look at the paintings of George Washington.

What makes the paintings different?

Listen to a subject in music, called a *theme*.

Stamitz: *Sonate for Viola d'amore and Viola* (theme)

Now listen to the same theme played in several different ways.

As each number is called, look at the chart.

It will help you hear many variations of this same subject.

CALL CHART 9: THEME AND VARIATIONS

1.	*SUBJECT*	*LOUD, FAST*
2.	*FIRST VARIATION*	*CHANGE OF RHYTHM PATTERNS*
3.	*SECOND VARIATION*	*SOFT, SLOW*
4.	*THIRD VARIATION*	*VERY FAST, MANY SHORT NOTES*

Stamitz: *Sonate for Viola d'amore and Viola*

Look at the paintings on the
next two pages. Can you *see* which painting
has a center of interest? Some music has focus.
Some does not. Can you hear which piece of music has focus?

Handel: *Water Music,* "Air"

Ives: *The Cage*

In painting, *focus* refers to a
center of interest for your
eyes to see. In music, *focus* refers to a
sound for your ears to hear.

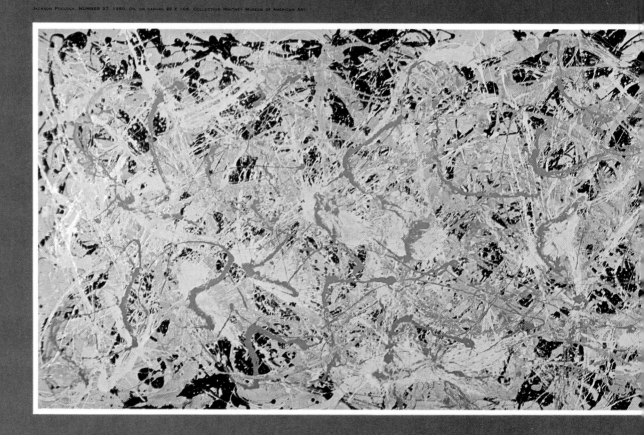

Jackson Pollock. NUMBER 27, 1950. Oil on canvas 49 X 106. Collection Whitney Museum of American Art.

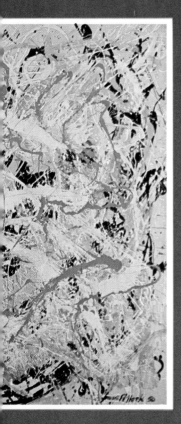

BALLA, GIACOMO. STREET LIGHT (LAMPADA STUDIO DI LUCE) 1909. OIL ON CANVAS, 68¾ x 45¼".
COLLECTION, THE MUSEUM OF MODERN ART, NEW YORK, HILLMAN PERIODICALS FUND.

Play the important tone on the G bell at the end of every verse of this song.

THE MAD MAN

AMERICAN FOLK TUNE   WORDS BY JEANNE WILHELMS

1. In old-en days there was a man
And he fell in a fry-ing pan.

2. The frying pan it was so nice
   And he fell in a bag of ice.

3. The bag of ice it turned to slush
   And he fell in a pan of mush.

4. The pan of mush it was so cold
   And he fell in a pot of gold.

5. The pot of gold it was so rich
   And he fell in a muddy ditch.

6. The muddy ditch it was so deep
   And he fell in a flock of sheep.

7. The flock of sheep did moan and groan
   And he fell in an ice-cream cone.

8. The ice-cream cone it was so sweet
   And he fell on his own two feet.

Play a bell part
throughout the song.
Try a different part
for each verse.

Notice the *focus* on the tone G,
both low G and high G.

You have played low G
and high G, an *octave*,
to accompany
"The Mad Man."

Now line up the bells
from low G to high G.
Feel the pull
toward the final tone.
You have played a scale.

Now line up these twelve
bells as shown.
You will need all the
bells except high G.

Feel that there is *no* pull
toward a final tone.
You have played a *tone row.*

Play upward.
Play downward.

It is *tonal* because there is
a *focus* on one important tone, G.

Play upward.
Play downward.

It is *atonal* because there is *no*
focus on one important tone.

This song is *tonal.* Can you tell why?

OL' CLO'   TRADITIONAL ROUND

FROM GIRL SCOUT SONG BOOK, P. 91 AS PUBLISHED IN 1925 BY GIRL SCOUTS INC.

My   un - cle   he   sells   ol'   clo',

He's   a   deal - er   in   chi - na,   you know;

And wher - ev - er you go, when you hear "Ol' clo',"

My un - cle is there, you know.

Now listen to the recording. Do you *hear* what you *see?*

To hear how the melody focuses on the tone G, take turns playing the G bell throughout the song.

Make up your own rhythm pattern.

This song is *atonal.* Can you tell why?

OL' CLO'

MUSIC BY DORIS HAYS

mf My___ un - cle he sells ol' clo',

He's a deal - er in___ chi - na, you know;

And wher - ev - er you go, when you hear "Ol'___ clo',"

My un - cle's there, you know!

Now listen to the recording. Do you *hear* what you *see?*

Listen to this old familiar song. It is *tonal.*

Can you tell why?

TWINKLE, TWINKLE, LITTLE STAR TRADITIONAL

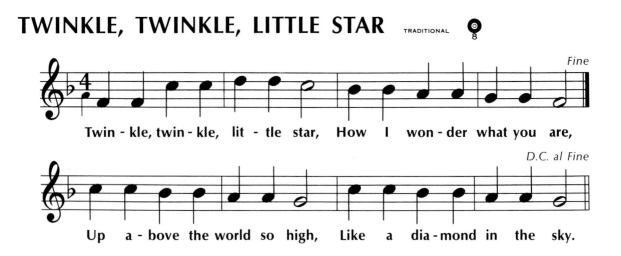

Twin - kle, twin - kle, lit - tle star, How I won - der what you are,

Up a - bove the world so high, Like a dia - mond in the sky.

Now listen to this "Twinkle, Twinkle, Little Star" song.

It is *atonal.* Can you tell why?

TWINKLE, TWINKLE, LITTLE STAR MUSIC BY DAVID EDDLEMAN WORDS TRADITIONAL

Twin - kle, twin - kle, lit - tle star,

How I won - der what you are,

Up a - bove the world so high,

Like a dia - mond in the sky.

WHAT DO YOU HEAR? 11: TONALITY

Some of the following pieces are *tonal* music.

Other pieces are *atonal* music.

As each number is called, decide whether the music is tonal, or atonal. Listen. Then circle what you hear.

---

1   TONAL   ATONAL   Handel: *Water Music,* "Air"

---

2   TONAL   ATONAL   Schoenberg: *Trio for Violin, Viola, Cello*

---

3   TONAL   ATONAL   Ravosa: *Love*

---

4   TONAL   ATONAL   Hays: *Ol' Clo'*

---

5   TONAL   ATONAL   Mozart: *Three German Dances,* No. 3

---

6   TONAL   ATONAL   Subotnick: *Touch*

YESTERDAY MORNING

FOLK SONG FROM COLOMBIA

ENGLISH WORDS BY JOAN GILBERT VAN POZNAK

FROM UNICEF BOOK OF CHILDREN'S SONGS, COMPILED AND WITH PHOTOGRAPHS BY WILLIAM I. KAUFMAN, COPYRIGHT 1970 BY WILLIAM I. KAUFMAN, PUBLISHED BY STACKPOLE BOOKS.

1. Oh, yes-ter-day at morn-ing, And then to-day at dawn,

Oh, yes-ter-day at morn-ing, And then to-day at dawn,

The tur-tle-doves were sing-ing, The roost-ers sang a-long,

REFRAIN

Ki - ki - ri, ki - ki - ri, I'm hap-py as can be;

Ki - ki - ri, ki - ki - ri, But who a-wak-en'd me?

2. The dogs for miles and miles ⎰(2 times)
Were barking at the moon, ⎱

A silly goose was cackling,

And thought she sang a tune, *Refrain*

3. A heavy rain was falling, ⎰(2 times)
And when it rains it pours, ⎱

With thunder, wind and lightning,

I wish I had some oars, *Refrain*

How many sounds do the maracas play for each of the drum beats?

Which instrument will you play

to accompany the song "Yesterday Morning"?

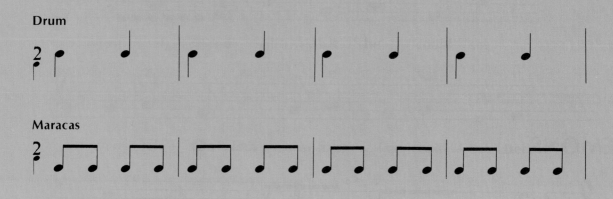

Drum

Maracas

Listen to the instruments that accompany the song "Lemons"

on page 170. How many can you hear?

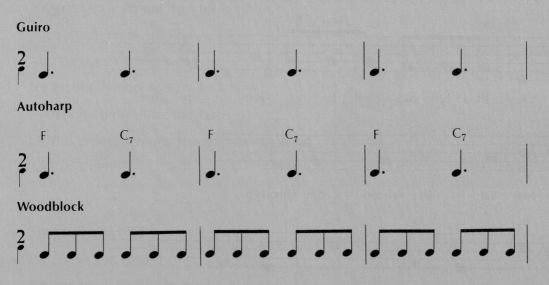

Guiro

Autoharp

Woodblock

Which instruments play the beat?

Which instrument plays the beat divided in three?

Take turns playing one of the parts with the recording as others sing.

Find the sign that shows that each measure has two beats.

Find space
in the room
to gallop.
Play the
pattern
made by
the sound of
galloping feet.

Find the pattern below.

1.

2.

3.

Now hear all three
patterns in
this music.

Anonymous:
Dadme Albricias, Híjos d'Eva

METER GAMES

Choose one of the games to play.

To play either game, choose a partner.
You play the boxes in one direction and your partner plays
in the other direction at the same time.

The numbers in the boxes
tell you how many sounds to play for each beat.

Follow the arrows and play the boxes,
going first in one direction, then in the other.

When there are two boxes side by side, play either one or the other.

You will need to set a steady beat before you begin!

If both of you make the same choice when you reach the boxes
at the end, *you* win a point.
If you choose different boxes, your partner wins a point.
After five games, count up your points.

Another time, try the other game.

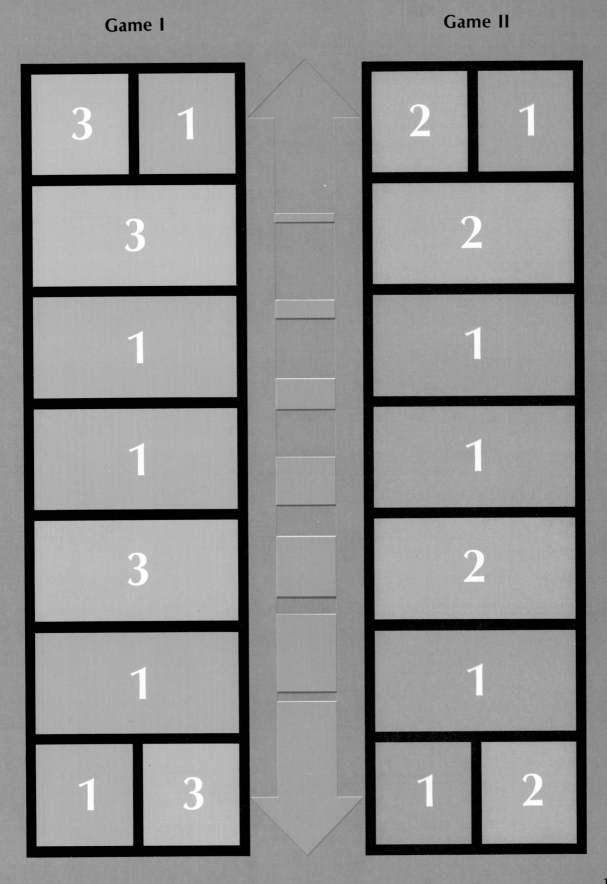

THE WEE FALORIE MAN

FOLK SONG FROM IRELAND   COLLECTED BY DAVID HAMMOND

1. I am the wee Fa - lo - rie man,
2. I am a good old work - in' man,

A rat - tlin', rov - in' I - rish - man,
Each day I carry my wee tin can,

7 I can do all that ev - er you can,
A large pen - ny bap and a clipe___ of ham,

For I am the wee Fa - lo - rie man.
7 I am a good old work - in' man.

3. I am the wee Falorie man,

A rattlin', rovin' Irishman,

I can do all that ever you can,

For I am the wee Falorie man.

THE OLD MAN

FOLK SONG FROM CANADA

FROM TRADITIONAL SONGS FROM NOVA SCOTIA BY HELEN CREIGHTON. REPRINTED BY PERMISSION OF McGRAW-HILL RYERSON LIMITED.

1. There was an old man came o - ver the lea,
2. My moth - er she bade me o - pen the door,

Ho, ho, ho, but I won't have him!
Ho, ho, ho, but I won't have him!

He came o - ver the lea I sup - pose to see me
I _____ o - pened the door and he bowed to the floor

With his long beard so new - ly shav - en.
With his long beard so new - ly shav - en.

3. My mother she bade me set him a chair,
Ho, ho, ho, but I won't have him!
I set him a chair, but I didn't care
For his long beard so newly shaven.

4. My mother, she bade me give him some meat,
Ho, ho, ho, but I won't have him!
I gave him some meat, but he wouldn't eat
With his long beard so newly shaven.

5. My mother she bade me sit on his knee,
Ho, ho, ho, but I won't have him!
For I sat on his knee and he tried to kiss me
With his long beard so newly shaven.

New things create a *modern style* of living.

New sounds create *modern styles* of music.

Follow the pictures as you listen to examples in modern styles.

guitar

○⊙
9 *Modern Sounds*

Hardin (arr.): *Lonesome Valley*

Arel: *Stereo Electronic Music No. 1*

Erb: *Phantasama*

Oliveros: *Sound Patterns*

Modern music has many different styles for you to enjoy.

small ensemble:

flute,

piccolo,

harpsichord,

string bass

English horn,

oboe

electronic
studio

Sing the chorus parts of "Hill an' Gully" to discover
how the tones move.

HILL AN' GULLY

CALYPSO FROM JAMAICA   ENGLISH WORDS BY MARGARET MARKS

REFRAIN

SOLO
Hill an' gul - ly rid - er,
CHORUS
Hill an'___ gul - ly.

SOLO
Hill an' gul - ly rid - er,
CHORUS
Hill an'___ gul - ly.

VERSE
SOLO
1. Took my horse an' come down,
CHORUS
Hill an'___ gul - ly.

SOLO
But my horse done stum - ble down,
CHORUS
Hill an'___ gul - ly.

SOLO
An' the night-time come an' tum - ble down,
CHORUS
Hill an'___ gul - ly.
D.C.

2. Oh, the moon shine bright down,

Hill an' gully.

Ain't no place to hide in down,

Hill an' gully.

An' a zombie come a-ridin' down,

Hill an' gully.

3. Oh, my knees they shake down,

Hill an' gully.

An' my heart starts quakin' down,

Hill an' gully.

Ain't nobody goin' to get me down,

Hill an' gully.

4. That's the last I set down,

Hill an' gully.

Pray the Lord don' let me down,

Hill an' gully.

An' I run till daylight breakin' down,

Hill an' gully.

180   Intervals

Sing the chorus parts. Which ones use only repeated tones?

Which ones use a leap?

OLD HOUSE AMERICAN FOLK GAME SONG   COLLECTED BY JOHN W. WORK

2. New house. Build it up!

Who's going to help me? Build it up!

Bring me a hammer. Build it up!

Bring me a saw. Build it up!

Next thing you bring me, Build it up!

Is a carpenter man. Build it up!

How does the melody work?

Do the tones repeat, move by step, or leap?

Play these melodies on bells or recorder.

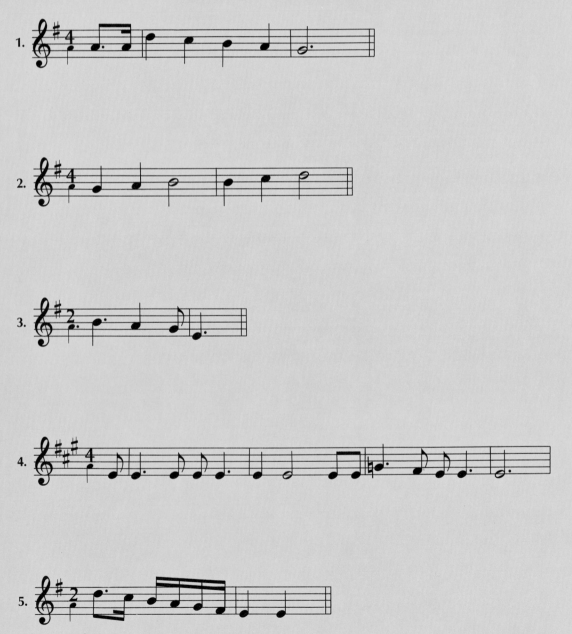

Follow the notes as you sing a song you know.

Does the melody move mostly by *steps*, or by *leaps?*

AMERICA

TRADITIONAL   WORDS BY SAMUEL FRANCIS SMITH

My coun-try! 'tis of thee, Sweet land of lib-er-ty,

Of thee I sing; Land where my fa-thers died,

Land of the Pil-grims' pride, From ev-'ry__ moun-tain-side

Let__ free-dom ring!

My native country, thee, Land of the noble free,

Thy name I love; I love thy rocks and rills,

Thy woods and templed hills, My heart with rapture thrills

Like that above.

Our fathers' God, to Thee, Author of liberty,

To Thee we sing; Long may our land be bright

With freedom's holy light; Protect us by Thy might,

Great God, our King!

Does the instrumental part move mostly by *steps*, or by *leaps?*

This patriotic song has steps, leaps, and repeats.

Listen for the two words "America, America" as you sing. On which one does the melody leap from low to high?

AMERICA, THE BEAUTIFUL

MUSIC BY SAMUEL A. WARD   WORDS BY KATHARINE LEE BATES

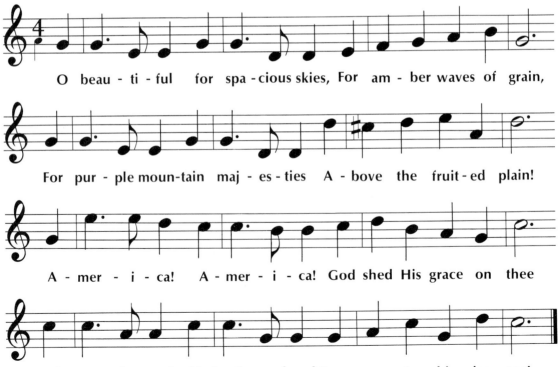

O beau - ti - ful   for spa - cious skies, For am - ber waves of grain,

For pur - ple moun - tain maj - es - ties A - bove the fruit - ed plain!

A - mer - i - ca! A - mer - i - ca! God shed His grace on thee

And crown thy good with broth - er - hood From sea to shin - ing sea!

Recorder or bells

(A - mer - i - ca! A - mer - i - ca!)

Find the notes that
begin the third phrase
of the instrumental part.
These notes are played when
"America, America" is sung.

Can you discover
how they move?

Follow the notes as you listen to this song.

Can you tell where the notes repeat, move by step,

and where they leap?

WONDERS NEVER CEASE
YIDDISH FOLK SONG

ENGLISH WORDS BY ELIZABETH S. BACHMAN

"HOB ICH A POR OKSN" FROM A TREASURY OF JEWISH FOLKSONG EDITED BY RUTH RUBIN. COPYRIGHT ©1950 BY SCHOCKEN BOOKS INC. REPRINTED BY PERMISSION OF SCHOCKEN BOOKS INC

1. I've a pair of ox - en, ox - en,

Ox - en who cut noo - dles, noo - dles.

Do you mean you've nev - er seen An ox cut noo-dles by the oo - dles?

Won-ders nev - er cease, Oh, won-ders nev - er cease.

Repeat these two measures for additional lines in verses 2-6.

2. I've a pair of bears, bears,

   Bears who sweep the rooms, rooms.

   Do you mean you've never seen

   A bear sweep rooms without a broom?

   An ox cut noodles by the oodles?

   Wonders never cease,

   Oh, wonders never cease.

3. I've a pair of goats, goats,

   Goats who wheel the children, children.

   Do you mean you've never seen

   A goat so glad to wheel a lad?

   A bear sweep rooms without a broom?

   An ox cut noodles by the oodles?

   Wonders . . .

4. I've a pair of dogs, dogs,

Dogs who write with ink, ink.

Do you mean you've never seen

A dog who'd think to write with ink?

A goat so glad to wheel a lad?

A bear sweep rooms without a broom?

An ox cut noodles by the oodles?

Wonders . . .

5. I've a pair of hens, hens,

Hens who gather wood, wood.

Do you mean you've never seen

A hen so good at gath'ring wood?

A dog who'd think to write with ink?

A goat so glad to wheel a lad?

A bear sweep rooms without a broom?

An ox cut noodles by the oodles?

Wonders . . .

6. I've a pair of birds, birds,

Birds who like to bake, bake.

Do you mean you've never seen

A bird who baked a layer cake?

A hen so good at gath'ring wood?

A dog who'd think to write with ink?

A goat so glad to wheel a lad?

A bear sweep rooms without a broom?

An ox cut noodles by the oodles?

Wonders . . .

These endings are called *cadences*. How does each one move?
Which cadence will you sing to end each verse?

Follow the notation as you listen to this song to discover that the melody moves upward and downward by steps.

This gives the melody its shape, or *contour.*

THE CAGE CHARLES IVES

A leop - ard went a - round his cage from one side
back to the oth - er side; he stopped_ on - ly when the keep - er
came a - round with meat; A boy who had been there three
hours be - gan to won - der,_____ "Is_____ life an - y - thing
like that?"

KOOKABURRA

WORDS AND MUSIC BY MARION SINCLAIR

FROM THE DITTY BAG BY JANET E. TOBITT. COPYRIGHT © 1946 BY JANET E. TOBITT. USED BY PERMISSION.

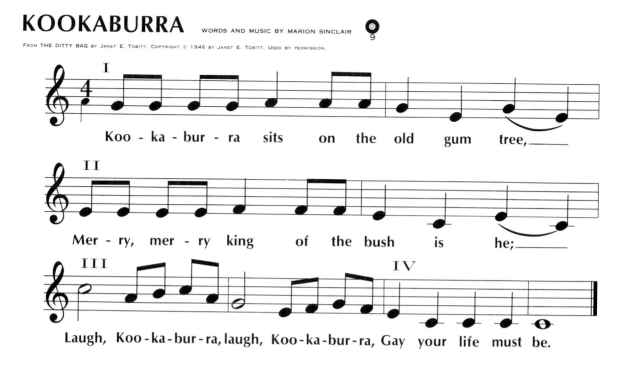

Koo - ka - bur - ra sits on the old gum tree,_____

Mer - ry, mer - ry king of the bush is he;_____

Laugh, Koo - ka - bur - ra, laugh, Koo - ka - bur - ra, Gay your life must be.

Bells or Recorder

1.

2.

Bells

3.

CALL CHART 10: CONTOUR

1. *STEPWISE*

2. *LEAPWISE*

3. *STEPWISE*

4. *LEAPWISE*

Tchaikovsky: *Symphony No. 6*, Movement 1
Webern: *Five Pieces for Orchestra*
The Wongga
Debussy: "Golliwog's Cakewalk"

Play these parts on the bells.

1. And had to be car - ried home in a cab.

2. Sab-bath, for a spe - cial treat, there's a 'ta - ter pud - ding!

3. Would - n't it be chill - y with no skin on!

4. Boil them cab-bage down, down.

5. Ah, 'tis true! Ah, 'tis true!

6. All the pret - ty lit - tle hors - es.

Listen to these melodies as you follow the notes.

Do the tones move mostly by step, mostly by leap,

or mostly by repeated tones?

As you hear each number called, look at the chart to help you.

CALL CHART 11: INTERVALS

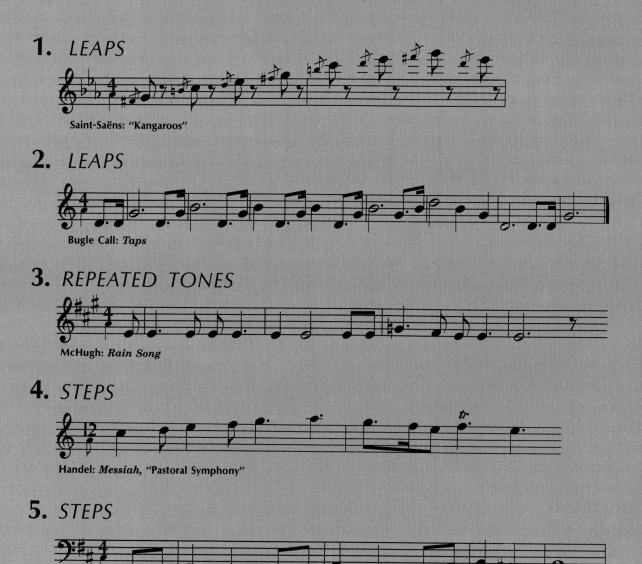

1. *LEAPS*

Saint-Saëns: "Kangaroos"

2. *LEAPS*

Bugle Call: *Taps*

3. *REPEATED TONES*

McHugh: *Rain Song*

4. *STEPS*

Handel: *Messiah*, "Pastoral Symphony"

5. *STEPS*

Tchaikovsky: *Symphony No. 6*, Movement 1

1.

2.

3.

There are many ways
to get an idea for the
contour of a melody.

One way is
to look at the
contour of a picture.

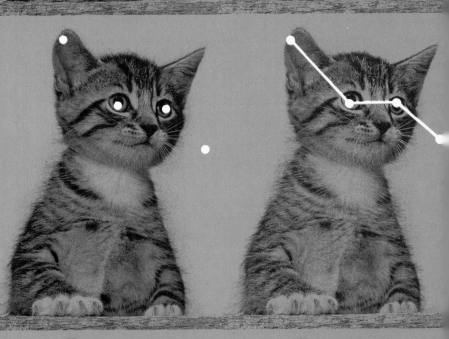

How does
the picture in
Column 1 change
in Columns 2 and 3?

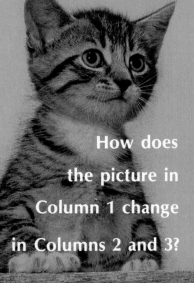

SOUND PIECE 5: Picture Piece

DAVID S. WALKER

Here are some contour lines taken from the ideas
in Columns 1, 2, and 3.

Play the tones they suggest to you, on bells
or on a piano.

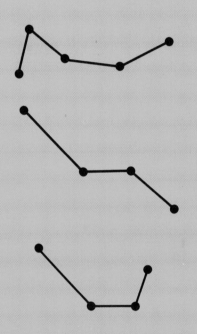

Will you use a steady beat, or no beat?

Will your piece be fast, or slow?

Will you use short sounds, long sounds, or both?

Will your piece move in twos, or threes?

Will it be loud, soft, or will the dynamics change?

Make up your own Sound Piece, using some of these ideas.

How do the notes move in this song?

MY TWENTY PENNIES

FOLK SONG FROM VENEZUELA   TRANSLATION BY J. OLCUTT SANDERS

1. With twen-ty pen-nies, with twen-ty pen-nies,

With twen-ty pen-nies I bought a *pa - va.*

The *pa - va* had a *pa-vi - to,*

I have the *pa - va* and the *pa-vi - to;*

And so I still have my twen-ty pen-nies.

*Repeat for additional lines in verses 2–6.

2. With twenty pennies, with twenty pennies,

With twenty pennies I bought a *gata.*

The *gata* had a *gatito,*

I have the *gata* and the *gatito;*

I have the *pava* and the *pavito;*

And so I still have my twenty pennies.

3. . . . *chiva . . . chivito . . .*

4. . . . *mona . . . monito . . .*

5. . . . *lora . . . lorito . . .*

6. . . . *vaca . . . vaquito . . .*

Listen to the following pieces. Each time a number is called, decide whether the contour of the melody is mostly stepwise, or mostly leapwise.

Listen. Then circle your answer.

1 *MOSTLY STEPWISE   MOSTLY LEAPWISE*

Saint-Saëns: *Carnival of the Animals*, "Kangaroos"

2 *MOSTLY STEPWISE   MOSTLY LEAPWISE*

Ives: *The Cage*

3 *MOSTLY STEPWISE   MOSTLY LEAPWISE*

For Thy Gracious Blessing

4 *MOSTLY STEPWISE   MOSTLY LEAPWISE*

Webern: *Five Pieces for Orchestra*, Op. 10, No. 5

5 *MOSTLY STEPWISE   MOSTLY LEAPWISE*

Bock-Harnick: *Sunrise, Sunset*

6 *MOSTLY STEPWISE   MOSTLY LEAPWISE*

Debussy: Children's Corner Suite, "Golliwog's Cakewalk"

Which of these lines shows the contour of the phrase endings of "All the Pretty Little Horses?"

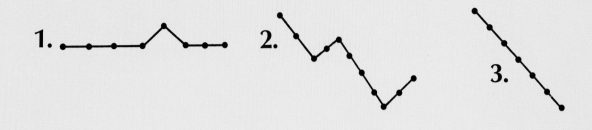

1.

2.

**Which of these lines
shows the contour of the
things you see in the pictures?**

These lines suggest the contour of a melody.

Sing or play a melody of your own that follows the lines.

SOUND PIECE 6: Sound Contours   JOYCE BOGUSKY REIMER

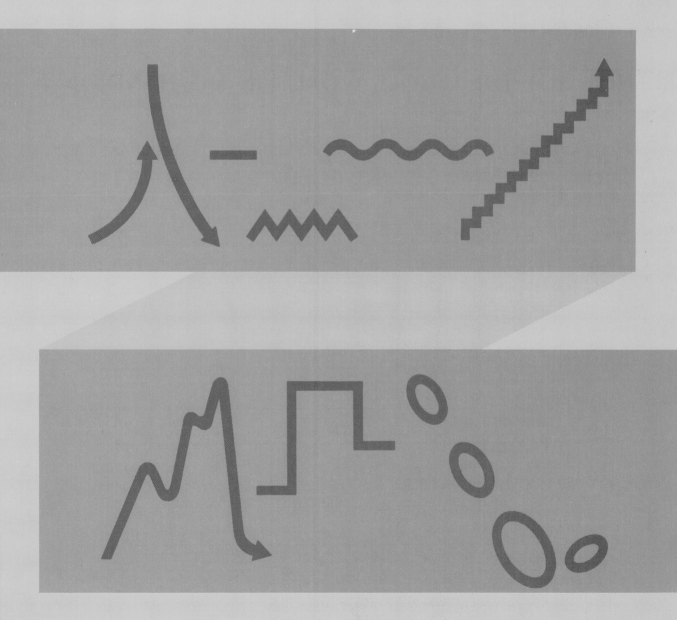

Make up your own sound piece using some of these ideas.

Sing this song as a melody alone. Then add harmony by playing the Autoharp chords.

HE'S GOT THE WHOLE WORLD IN HIS HANDS

BLACK SPIRITUAL

SAN SERENI

FOLK SONG FROM LATIN AMERICA   ENGLISH WORDS BY DELIA RÍOS

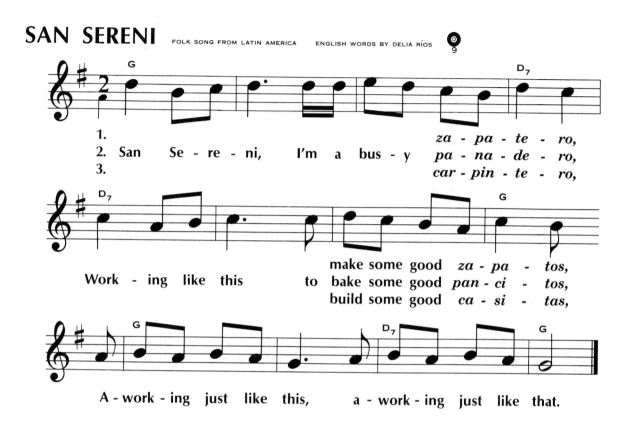

1.
2. San Se - re - ni,   I'm a bus - y   pa - na - de - ro,   za - pa - te - ro,
3.   car - pin - te - ro,

Work - ing like this   to bake some good *pan - ci - tos*,   make some good *za - pa - tos*,
                       build some good *ca - si - tas*,

A - work - ing just like this,   a - work - ing just like that.

Voices or Instruments

There is a familiar tune hiding in this song.

Can you hear what it is?

WHEN I FIRST CAME TO THIS LAND

WORDS AND MUSIC BY OSCAR BRAND

1. When I first came to this land, I was not a wealth-y man.

Then I built my-self a shack, I did what I could. I

called my shack, *Break-my-back.* But the land was sweet and good;

I did what I could.

*Repeat these four measures for additional lines in verses 2-5.

2. When I first came to this land,
   I was not a wealthy man.
   Then I bought myself a cow,
   I did what I could.
   I called my cow, *No-milk-now,*
   I called my shack, *Break-my-back.*
   But the land was sweet and good;
   I did what I could.

3. When I first came to this land,
   I was not a wealthy man.
   Then I bought myself a duck,
   I did what I could.
   I called my duck, *Out-of-luck,*
   I called my cow, *No-milk-now,*
   I called my shack, *Break-my-back.*
   But the land . . .

4. When I first came to this land,

I was not a wealthy man.

Then I got myself a wife,

I did what I could.

I called my wife, *Run-for-your-life,*

I called my duck, *Out-of-luck,*

I called my cow, *No-milk-now,*

I called my shack, *Break-my-back.*

But the land . . .

5. When I first came to this land,

I was not a wealthy man.

Then I got myself a son,

I did what I could.

I called my son, *My-work's-done,*

I called my wife, *Run-for-your-life,*

I called my duck, *Out-of-luck,*

I called my cow, *No-milk-now,*

I called my shack, *Break-my-back.*

But the land . . .

These endings are called *cadences.*

How do the tones move in each one?

Which cadence will you sing to end each verse?

THIS LAND IS YOUR LAND

WORDS AND MUSIC BY WOODY GUTHRIE

REFRAIN

This land is your land,____ This land is my land____

From Cal - i - for - nia____ to the New York is - land;____

From the red-wood for - est ____ to the Gulf Stream wa - ters;____

This land was made for you and me._____ *Fine*

VERSE

1. As I was walk - ing____ that rib-bon of high - way,____

I saw a - bove me ____ that end - less sky - way.____

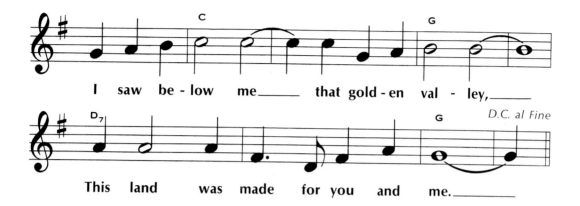

I saw be - low me_____ that gold - en val - ley,_____

This land was made for you and me._____

2. I've roamed and rambled and I followed my footsteps
   To the sparkling sands of her diamond deserts,
   And all around me a voice was sounding,
   "This land was made for you and me."

3. When the sun comes shining and I was strolling
   And the wheatfields waving and the dust clouds rolling,
   As the fog was lifting a voice was chanting,
   "This land was made for you and me."

Recorder or bells

Play a harmony part to a song you know.

Play the part all through the song.

7.

8.

9.

10.

11.

12.

Listen to the recording of "A Ram Sam Sam.

Follow one of the voice parts as you listen.

Will you follow the part for Voice 1, or the part
for Voice 2?

A RAM SAM SAM FOLK SONG FROM MOROCCO

Sing the melody of "America, the Beautiful" without accompaniment.

Follow the notes to help you.

AMERICA, THE BEAUTIFUL
MUSIC BY SAMUEL A. WARD   WORDS BY KATHARINE LEE BATES

O beau - ti - ful for spa - cious skies, For am - ber waves of grain,
O beau - ti - ful for pa - triot dream That sees be - yond the years

For pur - ple moun - tain maj - es - ties A - bove the fruit - ed plain!
Thine al - a - bas - ter cit - ies gleam, Un - dimmed by hu - man tears!

A - mer - i - ca! A - mer - i - ca! God shed His grace on thee

And crown thy good with broth - er - hood From sea to shin - ing sea!

Now play the recorder melody on p. 185 to go with

"America, the Beautiful."

This part is called a *countermelody*.

Add the accompaniment on the recording to your

singing and playing.

Notice how the added parts make the music sound thicker.

Listen to another version of "America, the Beautiful."

Is the density *thick*, or *thin*? Why?

Ward: *America, the Beautiful*
10

Listen to the recording to discover the *texture* in these songs.

The chart will help you by showing a drawing of the texture you hear.

CALL CHART 12: TEXTURE

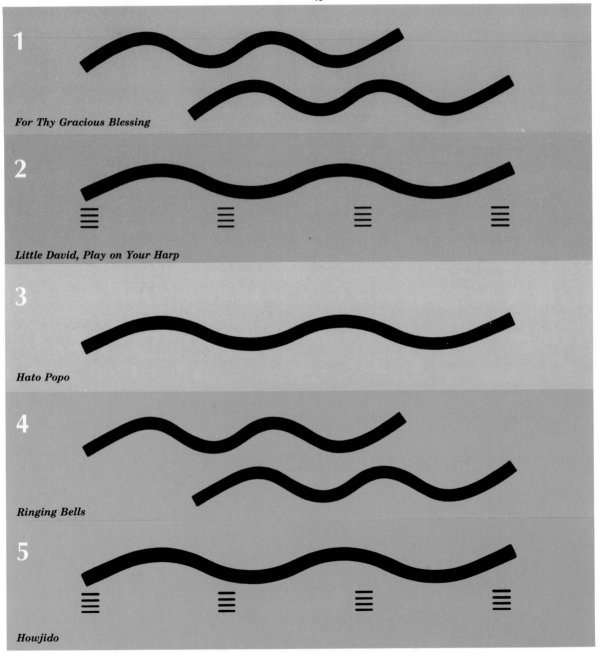

1

For Thy Gracious Blessing

2

Little David, Play on Your Harp

3

Hato Popo

4

Ringing Bells

5

Howjido

When each number is called, decide whether you hear *harmony*, or *no harmony*. Then decide what *tone colors* you hear. Do you hear voices, or instruments, or voices and instruments?

Listen. Then circle everything you hear.   Zynczak: *Love You*

---

1 HARMONY   VOICES
        NO HARMONY   INSTRUMENTS
        VOICES AND INSTRUMENTS

---

2 HARMONY   VOICES
        NO HARMONY   INSTRUMENTS
        VOICES AND INSTRUMENTS

---

3 HARMONY   VOICES
        NO HARMONY   INSTRUMENTS
        VOICES AND INSTRUMENTS

---

4 HARMONY   VOICES
        NO HARMONY   INSTRUMENTS
        VOICES AND INSTRUMENTS

---

5 HARMONY   VOICES
        NO HARMONY   INSTRUMENTS
        VOICES AND INSTRUMENTS

---

6 HARMONY   VOICES
        NO HARMONY   INSTRUMENTS
        VOICES AND INSTRUMENTS

Listen to two songs that children
in Mexico sing at Christmas.

Which one has harmony?
Which one has no harmony?

EL NACIMIENTO FOLK SONG FROM PUERTO RICO

San Jo - séy Ma - rí - a___ a Be - lén lle - ga - ron,___

Pi - die - ron po - sa - da___ y se la ne - ga - ron.___

Sing the melody alone.

Add harmony by playing Autoharp chords.

A min. A min. E₇ E₇ throughout

Add a countermelody.

Recorder or Bells

EL RORRO

CHRISTMAS SONG FROM MEXICO   ENGLISH WORDS BY VERNE MUNOZ

A la ru - ru - ru, ni - ño chi - qui - to,

Fine

Duer - ma - se ya,_____ mi Je - su - si - to._____

1. Now all the an - i - mals their si - lence keep,_____

D.C. al Fine

So they will not dis - turb the In - fant's sleep.

2. The choirs of holy angels from on high,
   Foretold the coming of this blessed child.

3. Oh, night of happiness, oh, night of joy,
   Guard well the Mother and Her Little Boy.

Recorder

Fine

B **Recorder, Violin, Bells**

D.C. al Fine

MELCHIOR AND BALTHAZAR

FOLK SONG FROM FRANCE   ENGLISH WORDS BY EMILY VIDAL

1. Mel - chi - or   and   Bal - tha - zar

Went up - on   a   jour - ney, Went up - on   a   jour - ney;

Mel - chi - or   and   Bal - tha - zar

Went up - on   a   jour - ney   far   with   King   Gas - par.

2. When they came to Bethlehem
They opened up the baskets,
Opened up the baskets;
When they came to Bethlehem
They opened up the baskets
They had brought with them.

3. Then they ate some cabbage soup.
They were very hungry,
Oh, so very hungry;
Then they ate some cabbage soup.
They were just as hungry
As they could be.

Play this bell part all through the song.

Bells

Each time a number is called there will be two pieces played. Sometimes the two pieces will come from the same musical family, or style.

Other times the two pieces will be from two different musical families, or styles.

If you think the two pieces are in the same style, draw a circle around the word SAME.

If you think the two pieces are in different styles, draw a circle around the word DIFFERENT.

Listen. Then circle what you hear.

1	*SAME*	*DIFFERENT*	*Idiophone Solo* Ravosa: *Love*
2	*SAME*	*DIFFERENT*	*Buying Fish* *'Taters*
3	*SAME*	*DIFFERENT*	Bach: *Suite No. 3 in D Minor, "Overture"* Bach: *Suite No. 2 in B Minor, "Overture"*
4	*SAME*	*DIFFERENT*	Debussy: *Children's Corner Suite,* *"Golliwog's Cakewalk"* Ussachevsky: *Four Miniatures,* No. 1
5	*SAME*	*DIFFERENT*	Mozart: *Three German Dances,* No. 3 Mozart: *Horn Concerto in E♭ Major*
6	*SAME*	*DIFFERENT*	Ussachevsky: *Four Miniatures,* No. 1 Hays: *Sound Piece No. 3*
7	*SAME*	*DIFFERENT*	Vivaldi: *The Four Seasons* (winter) Bartók: *Roumanian Dance No. 6*

Find the things that happened very long ago.

Find the things that happened not so long ago.

What is happening now?

Follow the dotted line to help you.

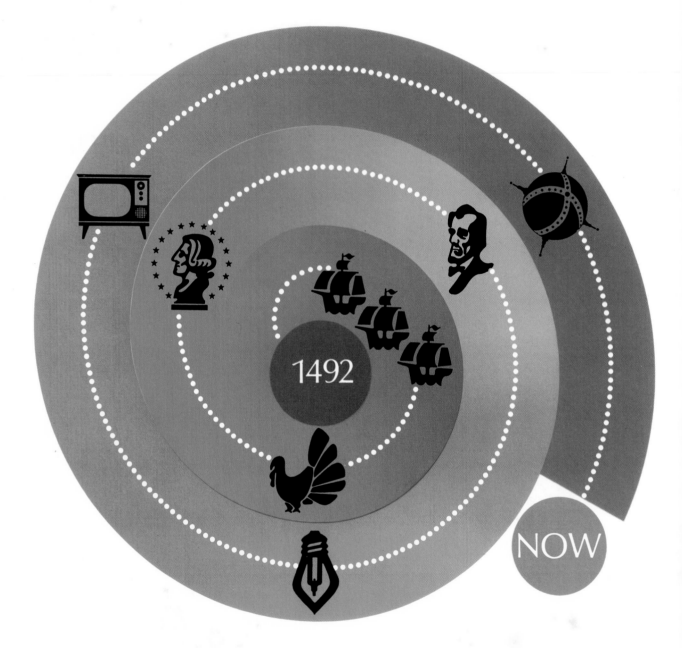

You have listened to music in different *styles* composed at different times. Follow the dotted line while you listen. Discover which instruments were used to help create different *styles of music.* Pretend you are a child living at one of these times. What musical style would you listen to? Listen to the piece you have selected.

1492

NOW

Chopin: *Scherzo No. 3 in C# Minor*
5

Anonymous: *Dadme Albricias, Hijos d'Eva*
1

Tchaikovsky: *Nutcracker Suite, "Trepak"*
4

Bach: *Passacaglia in C minor*
6

Baldridge: *Let's Dance*
6

Mozart: *Three German Dances,* No. 3
8

Ussachevsky: *Four Miniatures,* No. 1
7

RECORDER FINGERING CHART

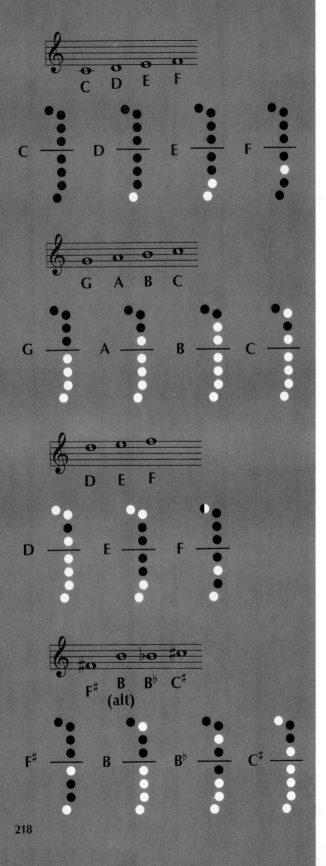

GLOSSARY

accent A single tone or chord louder than those around it

accompaniment Music that supports the sound of a solo performer

atonal Music in which no single tone is a "home base" or "resting place"

beat A repeating pulse that can be felt in some music

cadence A group of chords or notes at the end of a phrase or piece that gives a feeling of pausing or finishing

chord Three or more different tones played or sung together

composer A person who makes up pieces of music by putting sounds together in his or her own way

contrast Two or more things that are different. In music, slow is a *contrast* to fast; section A is a *contrast* to section B.

countermelody A melody that is played or sung at the same time as the main melody

density The thickness or thinness of sound

dynamics The loudness and softness of sound

form The overall plan of a piece of music

harmony Two or more tones sounding at the same time

melody A line of single tones that move upward, downward, or repeat

meter The way the beats of music are grouped, often in sets of two or in sets of three

notes Symbols for sound in music

octave The distance of eight steps from one tone to another has the same letter name. On the staff these steps are shown by the lines and spaces. When notes are an octave apart, there are eight lines and spaces from one note to the other.

phrase A musical "sentence." Each *phrase* expresses one thought. Music is made up of *phrases* that follow one another in a way that sounds right.

pitch The highness or lowness of a tone

register The pitch location of a group of tones (*see* pitch). If the group of tones are all high sounds, they are in a high *register*. If the group of tones are all low sounds, they are in a low *register*.

repetition Music that is the same, or almost the same, as music that was heard earlier

rests Symbols for silences in music

rhythm pattern A pattern of long and short sounds

tempo The speed of the beat in a piece of music (*see* beat)

texture The way melody and harmony go together: a melody alone, two or more melodies together, or a melody with chords

theme An important melody that occurs several times in a piece of music

tonal Music that focuses on one tone that is more important than the others—a "home base" or "resting" tone

tone color The special sound that makes one instrument or voice sound different from another

variation Music that is repeated but changed in some important way

vibration Back-and-forth motion that makes sound

INDEX

POEMS

SOUND PIECES

PICTURE CREDITS

3 4 5 6 7 8 9 10—RRD—85 84 83 82